AF008074

Better Tools for the Job

Specifications for Hand Tools and Equipment

by
William Armstrong
B.Sc., M.I. Mech. E., M.R.Ae.S., M.S.A.E.

Intermediate Technology Publications Ltd.

Practical Action Publishing Ltd
25 Albert Street, Rugby, CV21 2SD, Warwickshire, UK
www.practicalactionpublishing.com

© Intermediate Technology Publications 1980

First published 1980\Digitised 2013

ISBN 10: 0 90303 171 X
ISBN 13: 9780903031714
ISBN Library Ebook: 9781780441740
Book DOI: https://doi.org/10.3362/9781780441740

All rights reserved. No part of this publication may be reprinted or reproduced or utilized in any form or by any electronic, mechanical, or other means, now known or hereafter invented, including photocopying and recording, or in any information storage or retrieval system, without the written permission of the publishers.

A catalogue record for this book is available from the British Library.

The authors, contributors and/or editors have asserted their rights under the Copyright Designs and Patents Act 1988 to be identified as authors of their respective contributions.

Since 1974, Practical Action Publishing has published and disseminated books and information in support of international development work throughout the world. Practical Action Publishing is a trading name of Practical Action Publishing Ltd (Company Reg. No. 01159018), the wholly owned publishing company of Practical Action. Practical Action Publishing trades only in support of its parent charity objectives and any profits are covenanted back to Practical Action (Charity Reg. No. 247257, Group VAT Registration No. 880 9924 76).

Reasonable efforts have been made to publish reliable data and information, but the author and publisher cannot assume responsibility for the validity of all materials or for the consequences of their use.

The manufacturer's authorised representative in the EU for product safety is
Lightning Source France, 1 Av. Johannes Gutenberg, 78310 Maurepas, France.
compliance@lightningsource.fr

Contents

Acknowledgements	4
1. Introduction	5
2. Specifications	6
3. Tool Handles	7
4. Wheelbarrows	8
5. Tractors and Trailers	9
6. Procurement, Stores, and Inspection	11
7. Maintenance in the field	12

Detailed Specifications:

105	Shovel	14
106	Plain Jembe (Hoe)	16
107	Wheelbarrow (TU Model)	18
108	Fork Jembe	22
109	Crowbar	24
110	Trailer (5 tonne tipping)	25
111	Panga	28
112	Mattock	30
113	Shovel Handle	33
114A	Jembe/Fork Jembe Handle	34
114B	Pick/Mattock Handle	35
114C	Axe Handle	36
114E	Sledgehammer Handle	37
115	Axe	38
116	Pickaxe	40
117	Spreader (Rake)	42
118	Rammer	43

Acknowledgements

Much of the work involved in developing these specifications was carried out by the Technology Unit attached to the Ministry of Works (MOW) in Kenya in connection with their Rural Access Roads Programme (RARP). This work and the helpful co-operation of many division heads of the MOW, together with the various RARP Officers, has been of great value.

Permission from the Government of Kenya to publish these simple specifications is gratefully acknowledged. The publication should result in real help becoming available to other countries engaged in similar labour intensive projects.

We would also like to thank representatives of the British Overseas Development Administration (ODA) both in the UK and in Kenya for their willing help and support.

The principal overseas consultants to the RARP were Scott Wilson Kirkpatrick & Partners of Basingstoke, England. Their initial conception of the need for specifications to upgrade the quality of the tools and equipment, and the very considerable work performed on the basic drafting, formed the fountain-head from which this publication emerged.

1. Introduction

The simple specifications for hand tools and equipment contained in this publication and the various notes relating to them were developed in connection with the Kenya Rural Access Roads Programme. This programme is a Government of Kenya (Ministry of Works) project supported by the World Bank, the British Government, USAID, and certain other Governments. Started in 1975, the plan was to build some 15,000 kilometres of simple unsealed roads in remote parts of the country using *labour intensive* methods during an approximate 10 year period. It is anticipated that over 10,000 people will be employed at the peak. Besides helping to reduce unemployment the programme has socio/economic merits in opening up remote areas, thus stimulating agricultural production and aiding education and medical care.

It will be appreciated that such a project calls for the use of very large quantities of hand tools such as shovels, jembes, etc., and simple equipment such as wheelbarrows. At the outset of the RARP the quality of these items was, in general, very poor leading to breakages, supply difficulties, and low productivity in the field. The basic reason for this very unsatisfactory situation was the practice of buying tools and equipment by tender at the lowest quoted price, resulting in the provision of tools of poor design which lacked strength and durability.

Regrettably this same policy of buying at lowest tender price is common in many developing countries, and results in similar unsatisfactory performances when the tools and equipment are put to work in the field.

Attached to the Kenya MOW in Nairobi was a Technology Unit which among other functions worked intensively on the upgrading of tool and equipment quality. By the end of 1978 this work had drawn to a successful conclusion and the simple specifications and other data in this book record the information developed, so that it is now available for *labour intensive* projects of many types in other countries.

It may be added that insofar as the Kenya RARP is concerned, work done on tool and equipment improvement and the use of these specifications when buying has been a major factor in eliminating shortages, reducing wear and breakages in the field, and increasing productivity. Thus the work has been cost effective and hand tools and equipment are no longer a delaying factor in the programme.

2. Specifications

The full list of simple specifications 105-118 is given in the contents section at the beginning of the book.

It should be emphasised that these simple specifications are not intended to replace the more detailed national or international specifications such as BSS, SAE, etc, nor do they cut across the work performed by any Bureau of Standards. Rather, they represent practical and manageable information (together with simple drawings) which can be used commercially for buying, inspection, and testing, thus ensuring that the various items procured will be durable and give good productivity in service.

In order to obtain good quality durable hand tools the use of steel to reasonably controlled specifications is essential. The strength and behaviour of steel depends on its chemical composition (and heat treatment where relevant), and for this reason the required chemical composition of the steel forms part of each hand tool specification.

In the absence of a local steel industry much of the steel will have to be imported, a situation which applies particularly to the special alloy steel needed, for example, for axe manufacture (Specification 115).

At first sight the inclusion of chemical compositions in the specifications might appear to involve complications in the form of analysis for inspection purposes. Fortunately, however, there is a good correlation between the strength of steel and its hardness, and it is for this reason that hardness figures are included in each hand tool specification. The equipment needed for hardness checking (covering only 0.2% of items received — see section 6) is fairly simple and inexpensive and may be located in the store's facilities. Briefly, the checking process consists of pressing a diamond or hardened ball into the steel with a definite load. The diameter of the indentation gives the required correlation with the strength of the steel, based on standard tables.

Thus the need for chemical analysis can be reduced to occasional random checks, probably carried out at the local university, or similar institution.

It will be noted that each specification calls for the tool to be marked clearly with the specification number and the manufacturer's name and/or trademark. These points are important for keeping track of tools in the field and discouraging the introduction of low grade non-specified items.

3. Tool Handles

Experience in several developing countries has indicated that a very large proportion of the problems encountered with hand tools in the field (on road, irrigation, and construction projects, for example) arise from the use of handles made from cheap *unseasoned* softwood, coupled with poor manufacturing quality. Breakages, loose tool heads, and unsatisfactory grips are typical problems, leading to poor productivity and waste of time.

This is surprising since suitable hardwoods are widely available, seasoning can be carried out naturally if kilns are not in use, and there appears generally to be adequate manufacturing capability either by machine, or, in rural areas, by manual methods.

Thus the manufacture of tool handles to specification is a vital and relatively easy step in the upgrading of hand tool quality and productivity in the field. The cost increase for a "specified" handle as compared with a "cheap" handle is modest, and no other single step can return such high dividends in terms of cost effectiveness and productivity as the manufacture of tool handles to specification from *seasoned* hardwood.

It is for this reason that specifications 113, 114A, 114B, 114C, 114E, covering handles for various types of tools are included in this publication.

Suitable hardwoods will have specific gravity 0.66-0.80* after seasoning and will preferably be long grained. Seasoning should be to a moisture content of 20% maximum, either by kiln or natural means. Natural seasoning may take about seven weeks. In view of the very large variety of hardwoods in different parts of the world it is recommended that the selection of appropriate types for tool handles be discussed and agreed with the Government Forestry Department (or similar official body) in each particular country.

In some countries manufacturing industries may have special profile turning lathes available on which tool handles can readily be manufactured. However, rural skills should not be overlooked and satisfactory handles can usually be produced by hand in rural areas. It is important that seasoned wood of the appropriate type be used — not just a branch cut off a convenient tree! To this end it may be desirable to supply the rural workers with standardised blocks of seasoned hardwood from some central (probably Government) source. For example for the jembe (hoe) handle, specification 114A, the standardised blocks would need to be 950mm x 62mm x 50mm.

A word of caution about axe handles, specification 114C. The attachment to the axe, specification 115, is vitally important and includes a wedge for assembly. The manufacture of axe handles and fitting them to the axe heads is preferably a job for experienced specialists.

Note: Specific gravity 0.66-0.80 corresponds to 41-50 lbs per cubic foot.

4. Wheelbarrows

It is difficult to visualise any labour intensive project which does not involve wheelbarrows to a considerable extent. In the course of the tool and equipment upgrading work for the Kenya RAR Programme it proved impossible to find a wheelbarrow in East Africa with satisfactory strength and life expectancy, apart from one or two very expensive imported items.

Accordingly the TU wheelbarrow was designed and tested, using readily available hardwood for the handles and paying particular attention to the wheel/axle/tyre assembly — a major weakness in most designs.

The field tests proved satisfactory, the costs were economic (though higher than some local poor quality wheelbarrows) and the item was put into quantity production with local commercial organisations.

All this formed the background of specification 107 (including drawings TF5 and TF7), which shows the design and construction of the TU wheelbarrow in sufficient detail to enable it to be manufactured in any part of the world.

The tyre was made extra wide to give a good "footprint", and of solid rubber for ease of production and elimination of field maintenance (inflation) problems.

The two nylon/molybdenum disulphide plain bearings will almost certainly be imported (as in Kenya), but as they amount to only 1% of the overall cost this can be considered a very advantageous trade-off for the much easier "wheeling" when fully laden, and the greatly increased (maintenance free) life which results from their inclusion in the design.

Wheelbarrows with crude wheel/axle arrangements are difficult to push due to excessive bearing friction, particularly with a full load. This usually results in the operator only partially filling the barrow with consequent loss of productivity.

5. Trailers and Tractors

Many labour intensive projects, particularly in rural areas, involve the moving of earth, gravel, etc, in bulk over considerable distances.

Specification 110 covers a five tonne (hydraulic) tipping trailer developed in connection with the Kenya Rural Access Roads Programme. The specification is detailed and thorough yet the trailer involves no extraordinary skills as regards manufacture, although it is likely that the hydraulic rams and the tyres (with tubes) will have to be imported.

This development was an interesting and most constructive exercise with co-operation between the Kenya MOW, the Technology Unit attached to it, and certain commercial enterprises. The design proved very satisfactory on test and the trailer has been produced in quantity by three commercial firms. Field experience has shown that trailers built to specification 110 can be relied upon for good performance and durability under arduous operating conditions.

The appendix to specification 110 covers various matters which are important when trailers are being bought in quantity.

Since the use of the above trailers clearly involves tractors a few notes regarding the tractor/trailer combination may not be out of place.

a. *Compatability*

An important aspect of the combination involving attention to towing hitch, hydraulic reservoir capacity, load transfer (particularly on steep down grades), power to weight ratios, etc.

b. *Tractor Power*

Adequate power (including allowance for power drop-off if working at altitude) is a fairly obvious essential. Nevertheless it is also possible to overdo the tractor size with a consequent penalty by way of increased costs.

c. *Tyres and Tubes*

Tubeless tyres are completely unsatisfactory owing to air leakage following inevitable wheel rim distortion damage in service, hence the inclusion of tyres *and* tubes in specification 110.

d. *Hitch*

The hitch must be made from good quality heat treated steel, otherwise rapid wear will take place in service.

e. *Hydraulic Hoses*

Hose and pipe lengths and runs should be checked and any sharp bends or sharp radii should be corrected. Suitable clips and supports should be provided for hoses. Any sharp edges on which the hoses might chafe must be eliminated.

Leaking joints are an obvious but oft-neglected cause of hydraulic system problems.

f. *Hydraulic Disconnect Coupling*

This device automatically seals off the two sides of the hydraulic system when the tractor and trailer are separated. Per se the coupling is usually satisfactory but the danger of dirt getting into the hydraulic system is self-evident, particularly since the hose attached to the stationary trailer is often simply dropped on to the ground after being disconnected.

The drawing below indicates in schematic form a design to overcome this problem. It is, of course, essential that all components in the arrangement are robust, and also that operators are instructed to make use of the correct procedures!

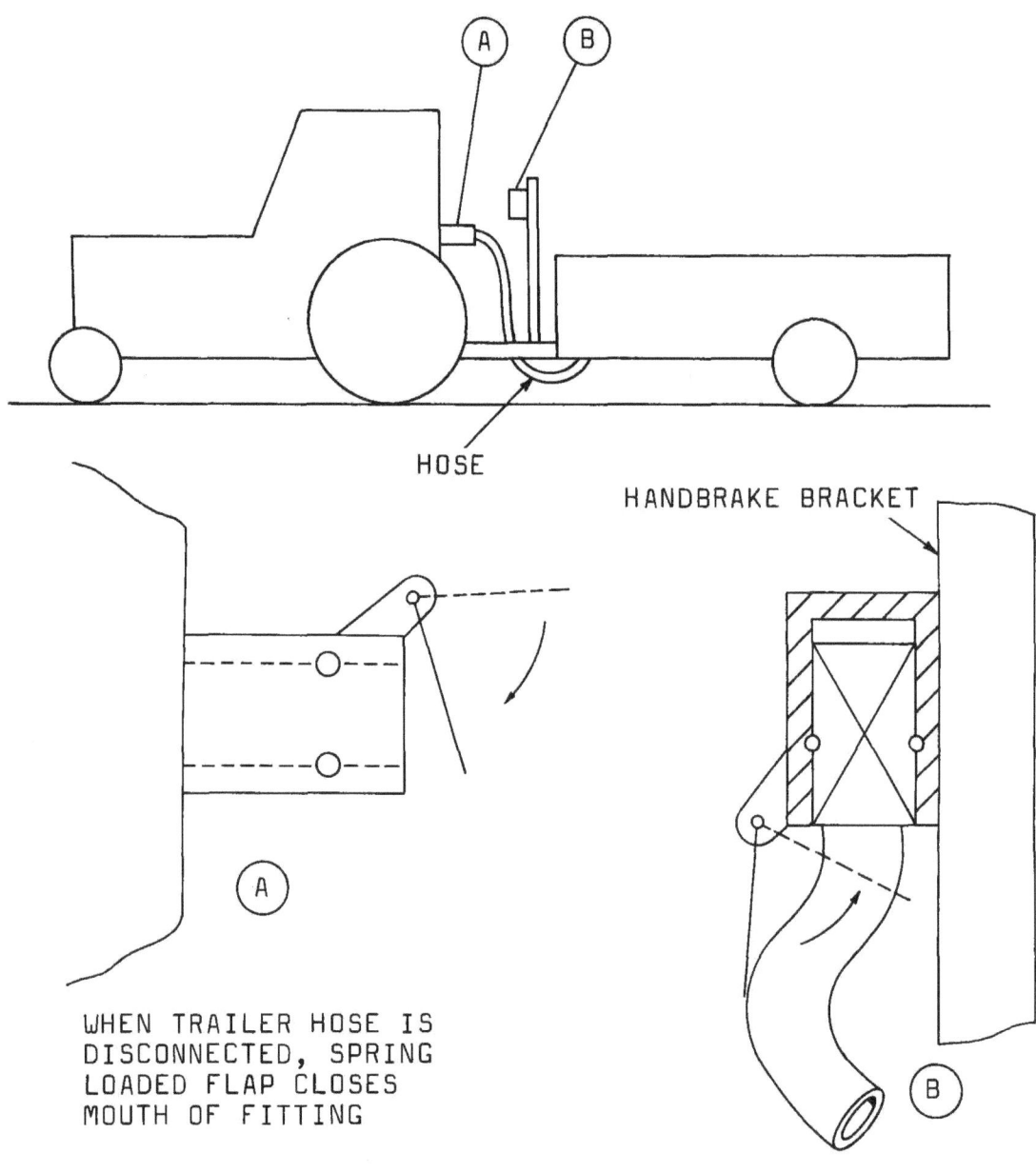

HOSE

HANDBRAKE BRACKET

Ⓐ WHEN TRAILER HOSE IS DISCONNECTED, SPRING LOADED FLAP CLOSES MOUTH OF FITTING

Ⓑ AFTER DISCONNECTING FROM TRACTOR, HOSE END IS PUSHED INTO DUMMY FITTING. THIS IS NORMALLY SEALED BY SPRING FLAP

6. Procurement, Stores, and Inspection

Although this publication sets out to deal principally with specifications for simple hand tools and equipment a few comments on the above subjects will be relevant.

Indeed, the initial function of the simple specifications is to accompany *all* requests for supply quotations from manufacturers (or importers).

If quotations are requested, for example for "1000 Shovels", there is every chance that the articles bought will be at the cheapest price — and quite unsuitable for service in the field!

If, however, the quotation requests go out as "1000 Shovels to specification 105 attached" the manufacturer (or importer) will have to ensure that the shovels are made from good quality steel of correct thickness, that the dimensions are in line with the drawing, and that quality in general is sufficiently good to pass the inspection tests.

Shovels bought in this manner will be more expensive (maybe 30%) than the unspecified articles, but will have an operating life probably 500% longer, besides considerably increasing productivity in service.

Thus the principle of "buying to specification" can be regarded as very cost effective.

As regards stores, the efficiency of any labour intensive project will be greatly increased by the provision of proper tool storage facilities and effective systems for the control of receiving (including inspection) and issuing to the field.

Before tools are put into stores it is, of course, essential that they be inspected to ensure that they are in line with the drawings and to specification generally. Thus the use of the simple specifications at "receiving inspection" becomes a second major aspect of their value. It will be noted that each specification has a drawing attached and includes a simple mechanical test procedure. In the case of hand tools a hardness checking figure is also indicated, to which reference was made earlier in Section 2.

It is felt that the following percentage checks at stores receiving will generally be adequate:

Hardness	0.2%
Strength	0.2%
Dimensional	0.4%

Thus taking a batch of 1000 shovels or jembes the quantities for checking, selected at random, would be two for strength, two for hardness, and four for dimensions. This checking will (or should be) virtually non-destructive.

7. Maintenance in the Field

Although this subject is not directly related to the matter of specifications a few notes may be useful.

Assuming the specifications have been used for procurement and inspection into central stores there will be available for the particular project (road construction, irrigation, etc) a supply of good quality durable tools and simple equipment.

The field performance (life and productivity) will, as pointed out earlier, be greatly superior to that of unspecified "cheap" tools and equipment. This performance can be extended by the provision of elementary maintenance and repair facilities at field camps under the general control and supervision of the foreman. The basic equipment involved is simple and low priced, although the type will depend on the availability or otherwise of a supply of electricity.

Such "self-help" jobs as sharpening of jembes using honing stones, fitting of new handles to shovels etc, repairs to wheelbarrows, riveting of new panga handles, and similar elementary maintenance work should be well within the capacity of field camp personnel, and will be very worthwhile (cost effective) in extending the life and productivity of the good quality items which the project management has provided in the first place, i.e. has bought to specification.

A note of warning regarding welding. This is a job for operators who have had specialised training.

DETAILED SPECIFICATIONS

SPECIFICATION No. 105 — SHOVEL

Note: Medium carbon steel is specified together with a minimum thickness of 1.75mm. Thinner material would prove unsatisfactory in service. Heat treatment is not considered necessary. Handles must be made from seasoned hardwood and sizes to give satisfactory strength are indicated.

Materials

Blades to be steel to the following specification:

Carbon	Manganese	Phosphorus	Sulphur
Percent	*Percent*	*Percent*	*Percent*
0.40/0.50	0.50/0.80	0.05 max	0.05 max

Handles to be hardwood, free from defects, and seasoned to not more than 20% moisture content.

Construction

Blade and socket to be formed from one piece of steel 1.75mm minimum thickness, free from cracks or other defects. Hilt to be wooden T or metal Y (with wooden grip) as shown on Figure 2.

Strength and Hardness Tests

a. With the tool clamped as shown in Figure 3, a load of 50kg shall be gradually applied by suspension from the grip and maintained for two minutes. On removal of the load the tool shall show no signs of damage or loosening of any component part, nor shall there be any permanent set in excess of 25mm when measured at the grip.

b. Hardness of blade to be 190-240 Brinell B.

Marking

Shovels to be clearly and indelibly marked on the blade or socket with:

a. Manufacturer's name and/or trademark.

b. The figures 105.

SPECIFICATION NO.105   DIMENSIONS IN MM.

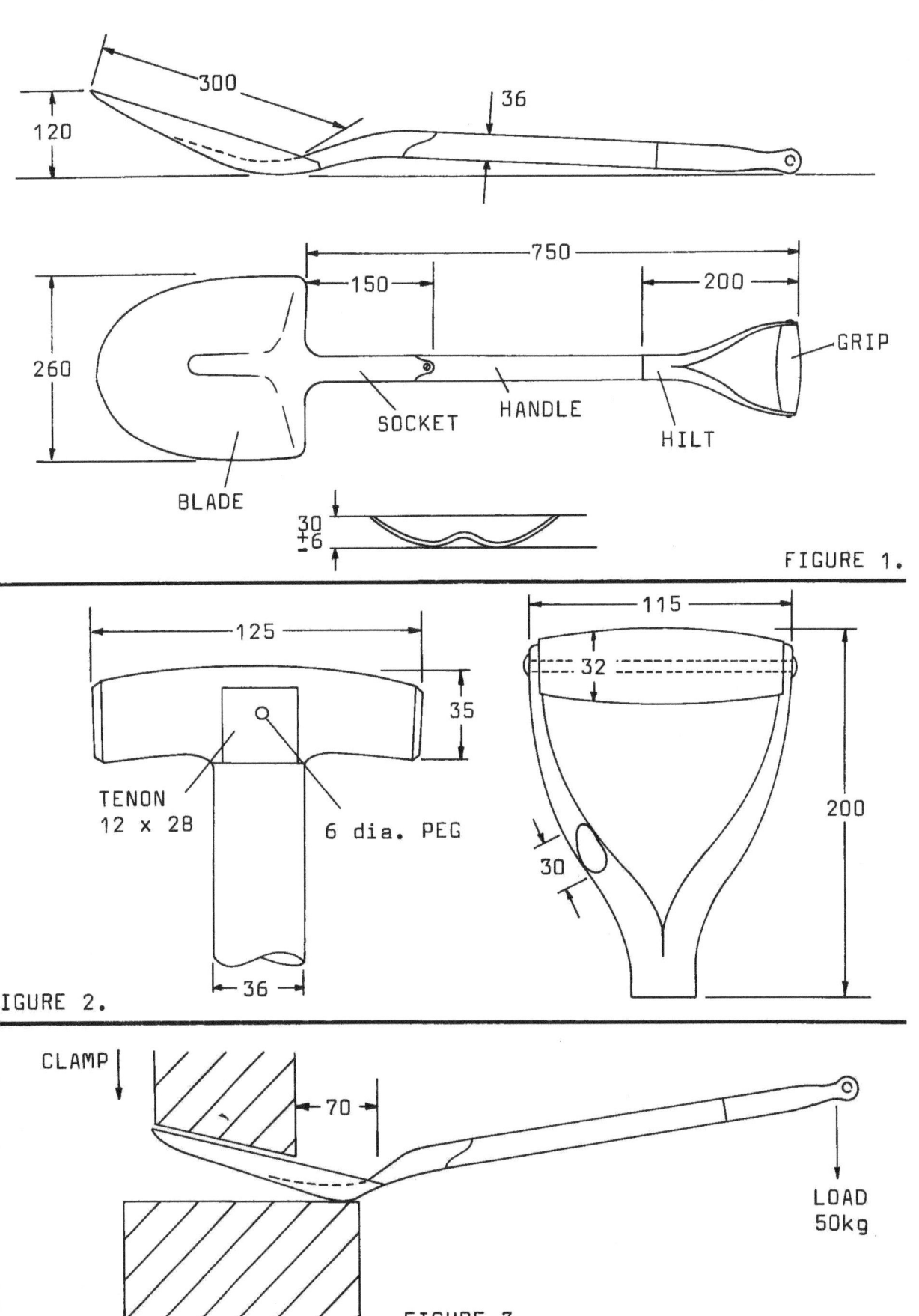

FIGURE 1.

FIGURE 2.

FIGURE 3.

SPECIFICATION No. 106 — PLAIN JEMBE (HOE)

Note: For effective life it is essential that this tool be forged from the medium carbon steel specified and heat treated as indicated.

Weight

1.5kg (+10%, −5%).

Material Specification (Steel)

Carbon	Manganese	Phosphorus	Sulphur
Percent	*Percent*	*Percent*	*Percent*
0.40/0.50	0.50/0.80	0.05 max	0.05 max

Heat Treatment and Hardness

After the forging has been normalised the lower part of the blade shall be hardened and tempered to give hardness within 50mm of the cutting edge of 40/46 Rockwell C. The hardened zone shall not extend nearer than half way to the eye.

Construction

The forging must be symmetrical and free from flaws. All fins and flashes must be dressed off. The eye must be smooth internally, uniformly tapered, and must lie centrally in the forging. The cutting edge must be ground sharp.

Strength Test

With a standard hardwood handle fitted and the tool clamped as shown on Figure 2 a load of 45kg shall be gradually applied by suspension at the handle end, and maintained for two minutes. On removal of the load the tool shall show no signs of damage to the head or loosening of the handle, nor shall there be any permanent set in excess of 25mm measured at the end of the handle.

Marking

The forging shall be clearly and indelibly marked with the following:

a. Manufacturer's name and/or trademark.

b. The figures 106.

c. The nominal weight.

Preservative Treatment

The head to be varnished all over.

N.B. The jembe may also be made of two-piece welded construction provided prior written approval of the design and material specifications is obtained. Such welded jembes must conform with all the requirements of specification No.106.

SPECIFICATION NO.106   DIMENSIONS IN MM.

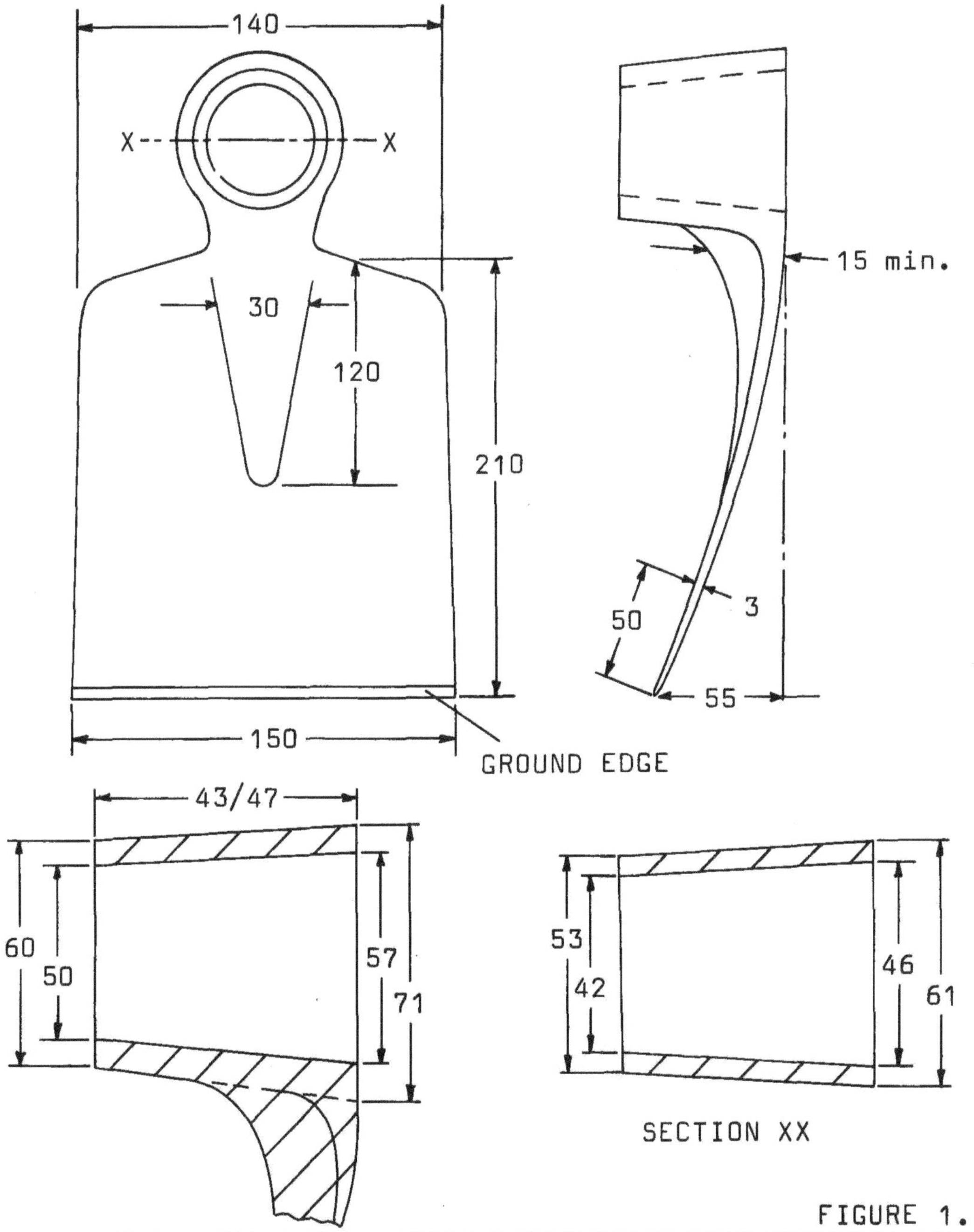

FIGURE 1.

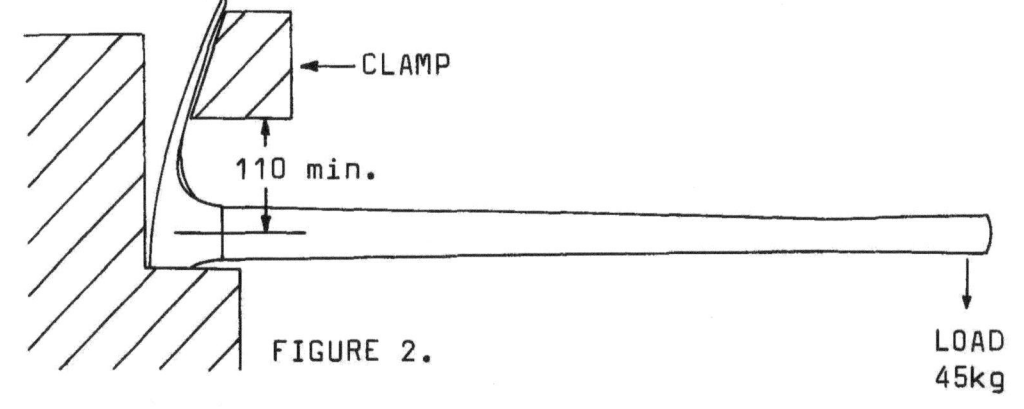

FIGURE 2.

LOAD 45kg

SPECIFICATION No. 107 — WHEELBARROW (TU MODEL)

Handles

Hardwood 40mm x 70mm, shaped appropriately at hand grips. Wood must be seasoned to not more than 20% moisture content.

Body

1.2mm (18 gauge) black iron folded and riveted, with 10mm reinforcing bar rolled into full perimeter of top edge. Struck capacity 70 litres.

Body/Handle Fixing

Four bolts, 10mm diameter, 100mm long, with washers 36mm x 1.5mm under "flat spherical" head of each bolt. Nuts with spring washers.

Legs

Two steel strips 6mm x 30mm bolted in place by body bolts. Two steel foot pads 5mm thick welded on.

Front Braces

Two steel strips 6mm x 30mm bolted in place with 10mm bolts.

Cross Brace

Two steel strips 6mm x 25mm bolted to legs with 8mm bolts 25mm long. Strips welded together at centre to form rigid X.

Axle

25mm diameter bright steel 220mm long, clamped to wooden frame by means of two steel caps 6mm x 30mm section and two steel load spreading pads 3mm x 30mm section, with 10mm bolts.

Wheel

Two 2mm pressed steel discs welded to tubular steel hub 36mm diameter, 145mm long, and clamped together by six bolts 8mm diameter, 12mm long, at 170mm pitch circle diameter. Two nylon/molybdenum disulphide flanged bearings 2mm thick and 25mm long pressed into ends of hub.

Tyre

Solid rubber 360mm diameter x 75mm wide. Tread pattern as appropriate. Inside diameter 220mm.

Marking

The wheelbarrow to be clearly and indelibly marked with:

a. The manufacturer's name and/or trademark.

b. The figures 107.

Treatment

Axle, two 2mm side thrust washers, and all bolts to have chemical rust preventative

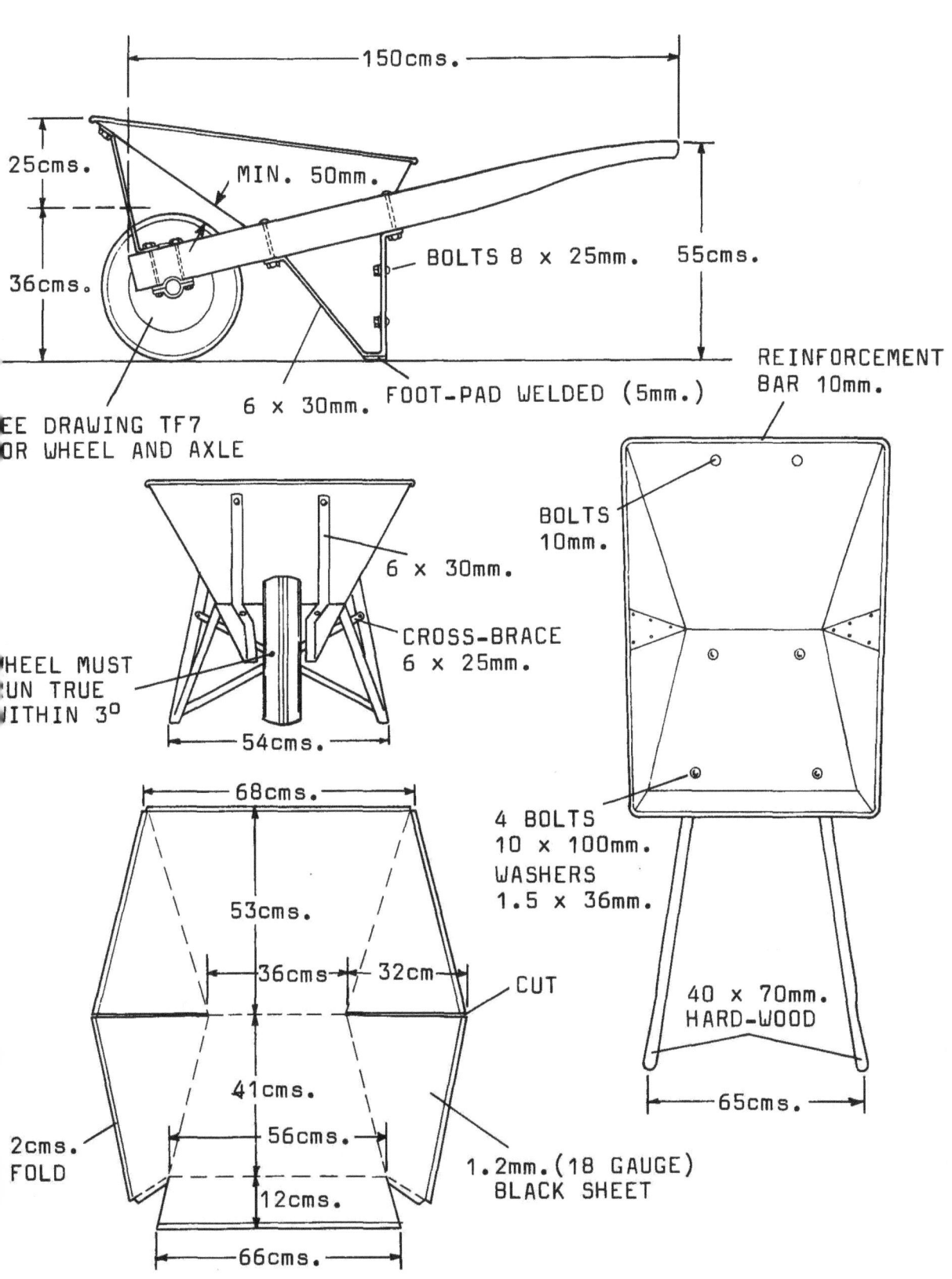

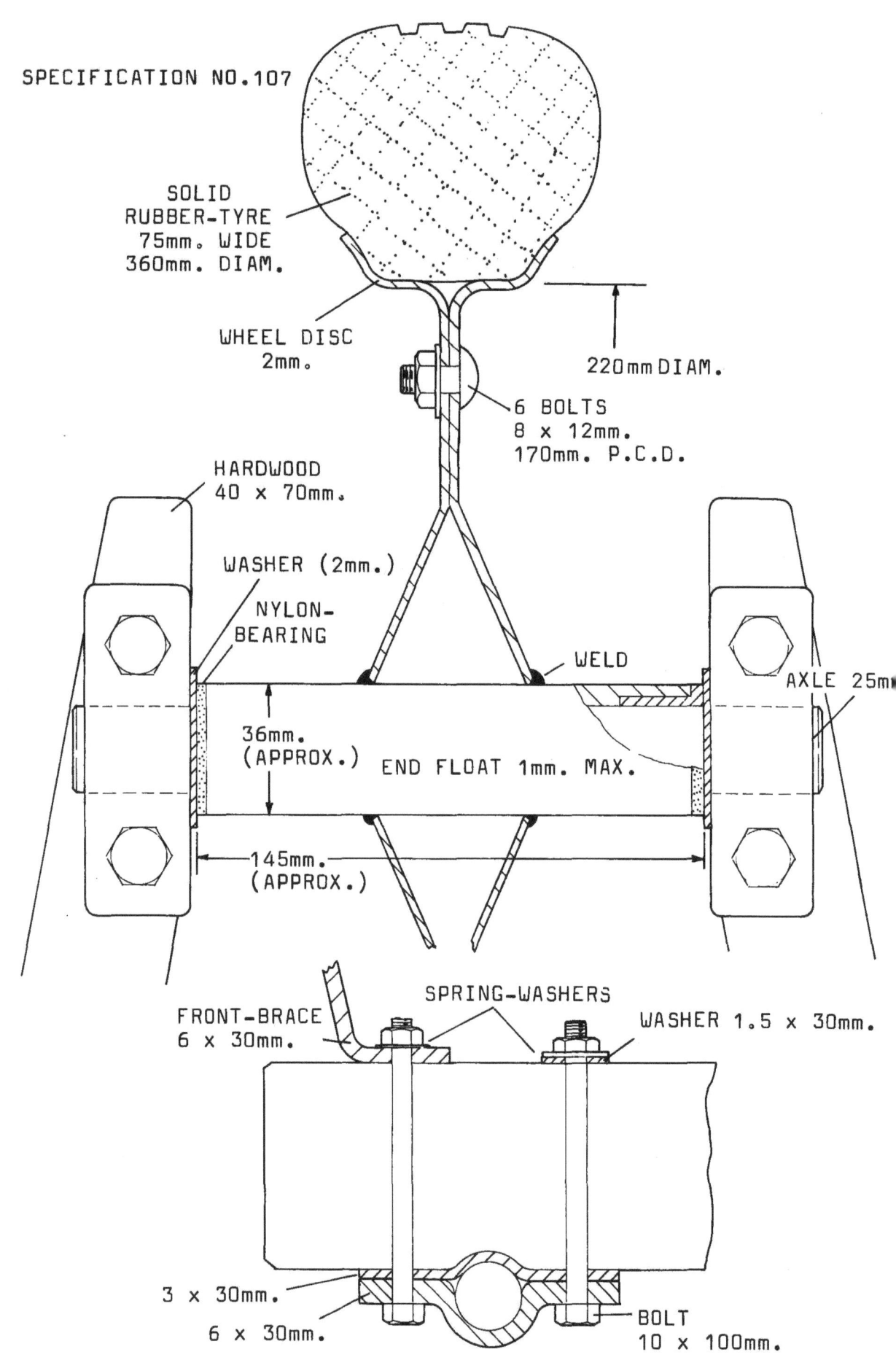

treatment before assembly. The wheelbarrow (with the exception of the tyre) to be cleaned, treated, and painted with one coat of preservative paint.

N.B.

a. Minimum clearance between tyre and body to be 50mm.

b. Two loose steel washers 2mm thick to be assembled between hub ends and wooden frames to provide endwise location of the wheel. End float to be 1mm maximum.

c. After final assembly the wheel and tyre must run freely and true within three degrees.

SPECIFICATION No. 108 — FORK JEMBE

Note: For an effective life it is essential that this tool be forged from the medium carbon steel specified and heat treated as indicated.

Weight
To be 1.5kg (+10%, −5%)

Material Specification (Steel)

Carbon	Manganese	Phosphorus	Sulphur
Percent	*Percent*	*Percent*	*Percent*
0.40/0.50	0.50/0.80	0.05 max	0.05 max

Heat Treatment and Hardness
The forging shall be hardened and tempered to produce Rockwell C 25/30 at the shoulders increasing along the prongs to Rockwell C 45/50 within 50mm of the tips.

Construction
The forging must be symmetrical and free from flaws. All fins and flashes must be dressed off. The eye must be smooth internally, uniformly tapered, and must lie centrally in the forging. The tips must be ground sharp.

Strength Test
With a standard hardwood handle fitted and the tool clamped as shown on Figure 2 a load of 45kg shall be gradually applied by suspension at the end of the handle and maintained for two minutes. On removal of the load the tool shall show no signs of damage to the head or loosening of the handle, nor shall there be any permanent set in excess of 25mm measured at the handle end.

Marking
The forging shall be clearly and indelibly marked with the following:

a. Manufacturers name and/or trademark.

b. The figures 108.

c. The nominal weight of the head.

Preservative Treatment
The head to be varnished all over.

N.B.
The fork jembe may be made by welding the prongs to an eye forging, provided prior written approval of the design and material specifications is obtained. Such welded fork jembes must conform with all requirements of this specification No.108.

SPECIFICATION NO.108

DIMENSIONS IN MM.

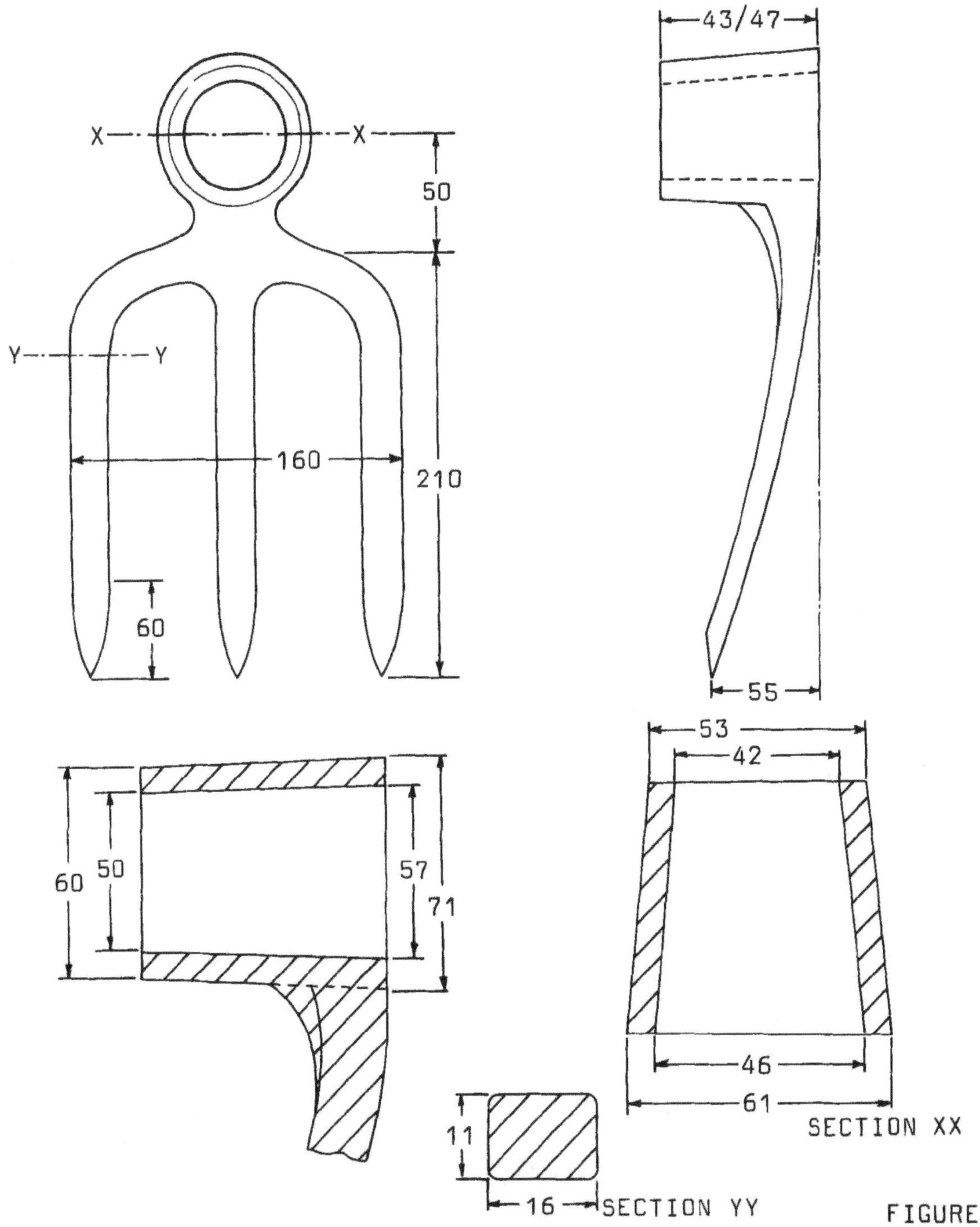

FIGURE 1.

SECTION XX

SECTION YY

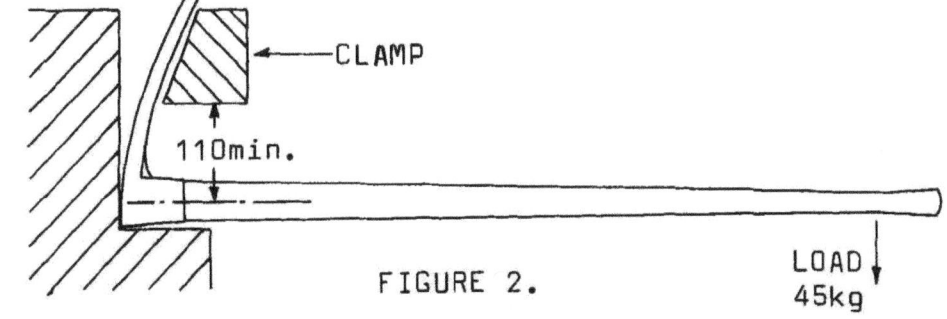

FIGURE 2.

SPECIFICATION No. 109 – CROWBAR

The crowbar is an essential tool in many labour intensive projects. Old scrap steel or concrete reinforcing bars are useless in the field. Crowbars made to this specification may appear somewhat costly initially but will be effective and long lasting in service.

Description

The crowbar to be 3cm diameter, 170cm long, shaped to a chisel form at one end and a four flat point at the other, as illustrated.

Material

Steel with 0.45/0.55 carbon content, hardened and tempered to give Rockwell C 45/50 when checked at four random points along the piece.

Weight

9kg approximately.

Marking

The crowbar to be marked clearly and indelibly with the following:

a. Manufacturer's name and/or trademark.

b. The figures 109.

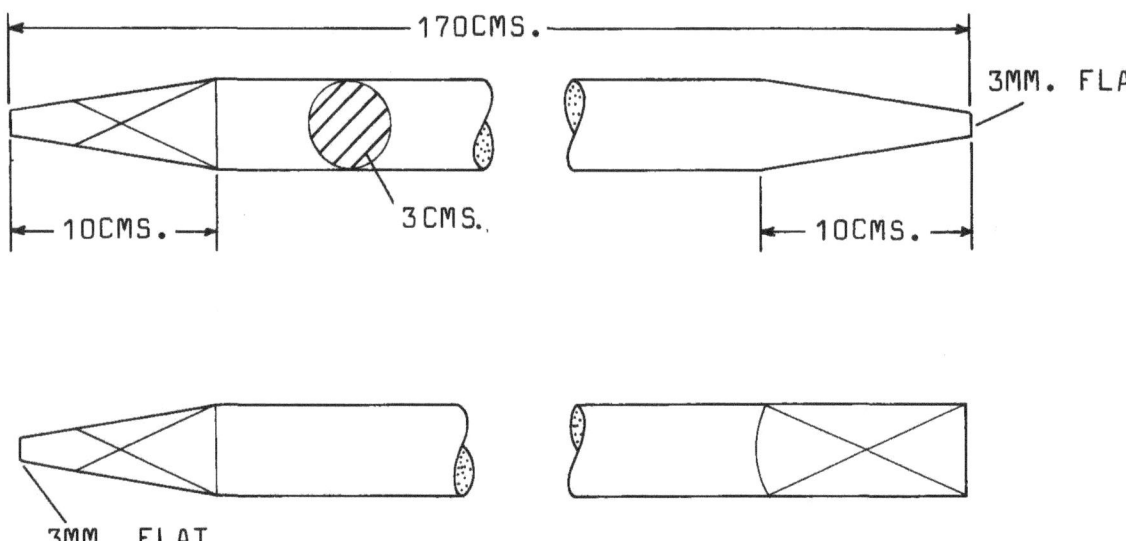

SPECIFICATION No. 110 — TRAILER
(5 TONNE TIPPING)

General

The trailer shall be designed for heavy duty operations with a single axle and hydraulically operated rear tipping body. The payload capacity shall be five tonnes and the struck volumetric capacity 2.8 cubic metres.

The trailer shall be designed to be compatible in use with a specified 45 HP tractor, fitted with automatic hitch, and increased hydraulic fluid reservoir capacity to ensure full tipping angle in service.

Dimensions

The maximum overall dimensions of the trailer body shall be as follows:

  a. Length 5000mm

  b. Width   2300mm

  c. Height 1250mm (measured at axle)

The axle shall be 70mm square (minimum) and so located that with the trailer fully loaded the load transferred to the tractor is 1.5 tonnes maximum/1.2 tonnes minimum.

The tipping angle shall be 60 degrees minimum.

A robust fixed skid type stand shall be fitted to the underside of the drawbar to enable the trailer to be hitched easily under soft ground conditions.

Construction details

The chassis shall be fabricated from 150 x 75 x 18kg per metre (minimum) hot rolled mild steel channel with 0.22% carbon (max), 0.8% manganese (max), and 30 tons per square inch/4650kg per square centimetre (minimum) tensile strength.

The chassis shall include a boxed cross member to support and guide the body. Such cross member shall be sufficiently strong and rigid to support the fully laden body without distortion.

The body sub-frame shall be fabricated from 100 x 50 x 10kg per metre (minimum) hot rolled mild steel channel to the same chemical and strength specifications as the chassis.

The body hinge pin diameter shall be 35mm minimum.

The body floor shall be fabricated from 2mm (minimum) **high tensile** steel plate with 18 tons per square inch/2800kg per square centimetre (minimum) *yield* strength, in the form of individual plates extending across the full width of the trailer and reinforced at centres not exceeding 200mm.

The body sides and head-board shall be fabricated from 2mm mild steel plate having chemical and strength specifications as the chassis.

The body sides shall be extended rearwards a minimum of 100mm to provide protection for the tailgate, hinges, and locking device.

The tailgate shall be hinged at the top with engineered hinges and heavy duty brackets, and shall be fabricated from 3mm mild steel plate having chemical and strength specifications as the chassis.

The tailgate shall be removable.

A robust locking device shall be provided for the tailgate operated by means of a lever located at one side of the rear of the body, and incorporating a full width cross shaft.

The towing eye shall be of alloy steel heat treated to ensure negligible wear over a two year period of normal service.

The cross member on which the ram acts when tipping shall be of sufficiently strong section to eliminate distortion in service.

Hydraulic equipment

The hydraulic equipment fitted to the trailer must be compatible with the hydraulic system of the specified tractor.

A dummy quick-release type female coupling shall be fitted to the trailer headboard, with the opening vertically downwards, in such a position that the connecting hose may be plugged in easily when the trailer is unhitched from the tractor. The dummy female coupling must be permanently fitted with a very robust spring loaded cap which automatically closes off the opening when the hose is removed.

The ram shall be high lift, two stage, and chrome plated.

Hydraulic hoses shall be single wire braid reinforced, and routed to provide maximum protection from damage in arduous service.

Tyres, wheels, and brakes

Tyres must be fitted with tubes and shall be 11.5 x 15 (minimum) with a 10 ply (minimum) rating.

Wheels shall be of very robust type with standardised dimensions for fixing holes.

Mechanically actuated drum parking brakes with minimum diameter of 250mm and minimum width of 45mm shall be provided. The operating cables shall be unsheathed and routed to ensure maximum protection under service conditions.

Painting etc.

The trailers shall be painted with one coat of red oxide primer and one coat of yellow gloss paint.

The trailers shall be fitted with reflecting chevrons and reflectors.

APPENDIX TO SPECIFICATION No. 110

Note: This relates to any tender for trailers.

Drawings

The following drawings are required:

a. General arrangement including side elevation, rear elevation, and plan (Scale 1:10 approximately).

b. Tailgate locking device (Scale 1:2).

c. Tailgate hinge (Scale 1:1).

d. Hydraulic quick-release coupling, including self-closing gap (Scale 1:1).

Special components

Manufacturer's printed specifications and relevant drawings are required to cover: cover:

a. Hydraulic ram and hoses.

b. Quick-release hydraulic couplings.

c. Axle.

d. Hub and wheel.

Warranty

12 months warranty against any problems or failures under normal operating conditions arising as a result of design, material, or manufacturing defects.

Price stability

The quoted price to be valid for 60 days from the tender closing date.

Tractor hydraulic coupling

The tenderer to be responsible for supplying and fitting quick release hydraulic couplings, together with self-closing caps, to the hydraulic systems of the specified tractors.

Spare parts

The following are required per 100 trailers:

    Tyre, tube, and wheel (20).
    Hub (complete) (5).
    Hub bearings (10 wheel sets).
    Wheel nuts (50).
    Hydraulic ram (10).
    Hydraulic hose (20).
    Quick-release hydraulic coupling with self-closing cap (15).
    Towing eye (10).
    Hinge pin (10).
    Brake cable (10).

SPECIFICATION No. 111 — PANGA OR MACHETE (46cm, HEAVY DUTY)

Note: The use of medium carbon steel and heat treatment as specified is essential to obtain a tool which will be effective in heavy service and will retain its cutting edge. Secure riveting of the hardwood handles is very important.

Materials

Blades to be steel with carbon content 0.52/0.60, heat treated to Rockwell C 40/45 when checked at three points along the blade.

Rivets to be steel with maximum carbon content 0.15. Washers to be mild steel.

Handles to be hardwood seasoned to not more than 20% moisture content.

Construction

Handles to be machine riveted to the blade at three places — see Figure 2 for details. Blades to be ground to sharp edge.

Test

With blade inserted in 10mm wide slot 150mm deep a deflection of 45 degrees in each direction shall be applied without breakage or permanent set — see Figure 3.

Preservative Treatment

Blades to be varnished and greased.

Marking

Blades to be clearly and indelibly marked with:

a. Manufacturer's name and/or trademark.

b. The figures 111.

SPECIFICATION NO.111

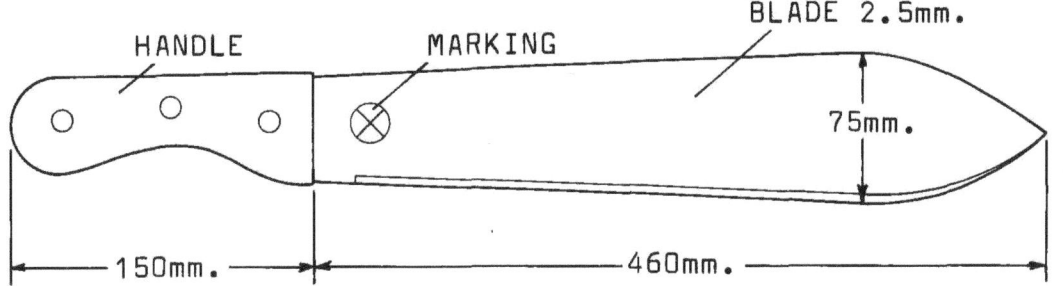

FIGURE 1.

RIVET 5mm. WASHERS 11 × 1.5mm.

FIGURE 2.

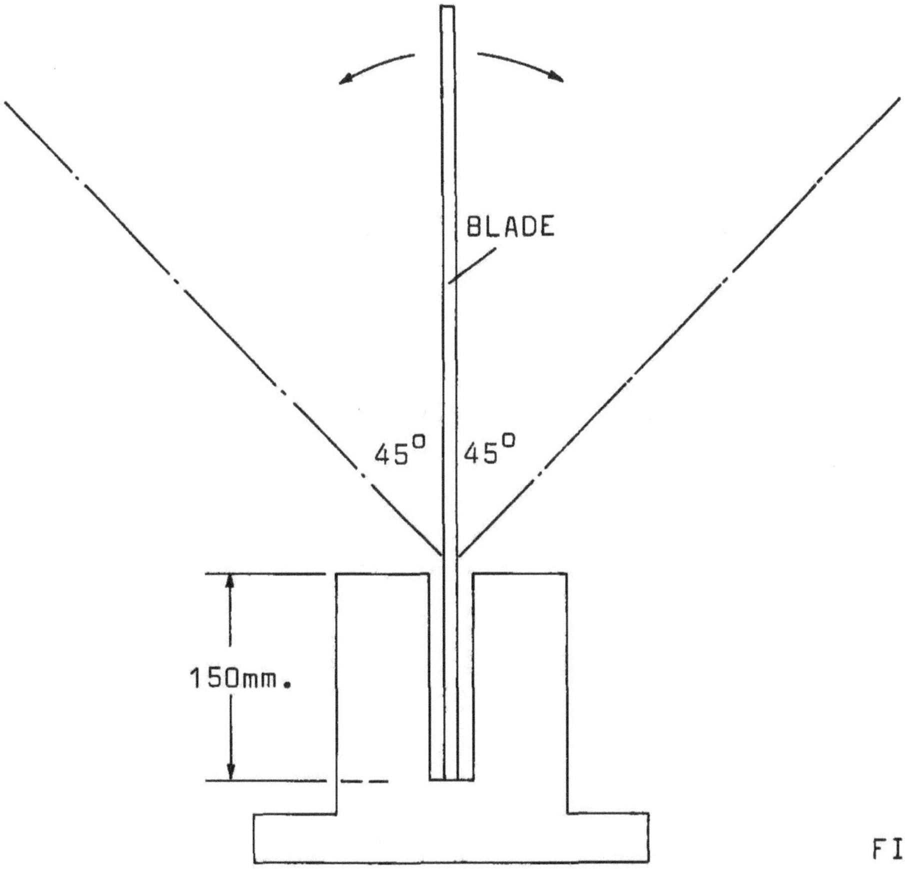

FIGURE 3.

SPECIFICATION No. 112 — MATTOCK

Note: It is essential that mattocks be forged from the medium carbon steel specified and heat-treated as indicated.

Weight

2.5kg (+10%, −5%)

Material Specification (Steel)

Carbon	Manganese	Phosphorus	Sulphur
Percent	*Percent*	*Percent*	*Percent*
0.40/0.50	0.50/0.80	0.05 max	0.05 max

Heat Treatment and Hardness

The forging shall be hardened and tempered to produce Rockwell C 25/30 at the eye, increasing to Rockwell C 45/50 within 50mm of the cutting edges.

Construction

The forging must be symmetrical and free from flaws. All fins and flashes must be dressed off. The eye must be smooth internally, uniformly tapered, and must lie centrally in the forging.

The thickness of the blades shall be greatest at the shoulders, decreasing towards the cutting edges which must be ground sharp.

Strength Test

With a standard hardwood handle fitted and the tool clamped as shown on Figure 2 a load of 45kg shall be gradually applied by suspension at the end of the handle and maintained for two minutes. On removal of the load the tool shall show no signs of damage to the head or loosening of the handle, nor shall there be any permanent set in excess of 25mm measured at the handle end.

Marking

The forging shall be clearly and indelibly marked with the following:

a. Manufacturer's name and/or trademark.

b. The figures 112.

c. The nominal weight.

Preservative Treatment

The head to be varnished all over.

SPECIFICATION NO. 112   DIMENSIONS IN MM.

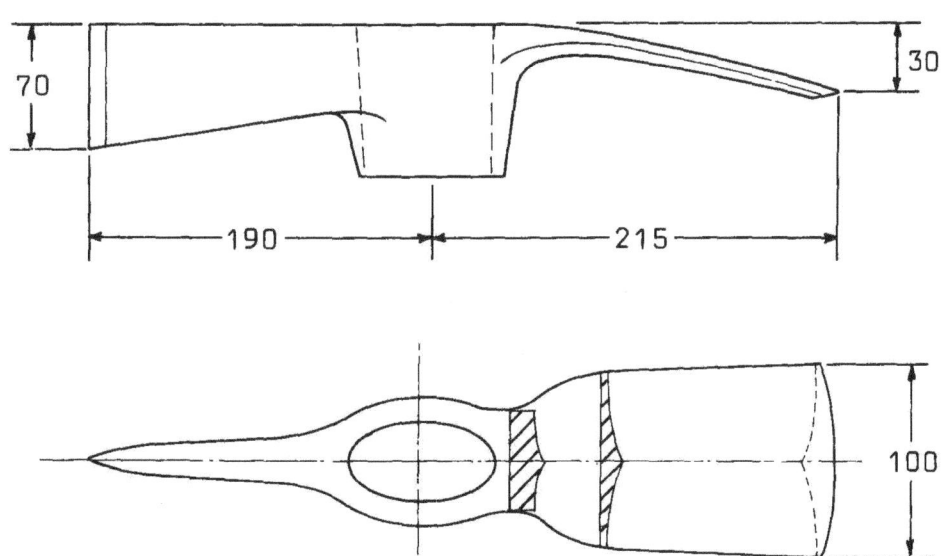

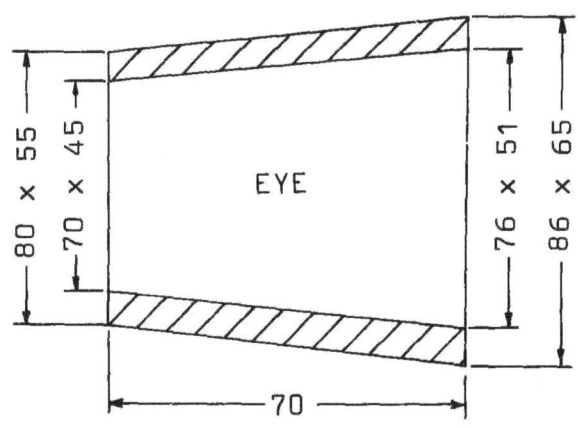

FIGURE 1.

SPECIFICATION NO. 112

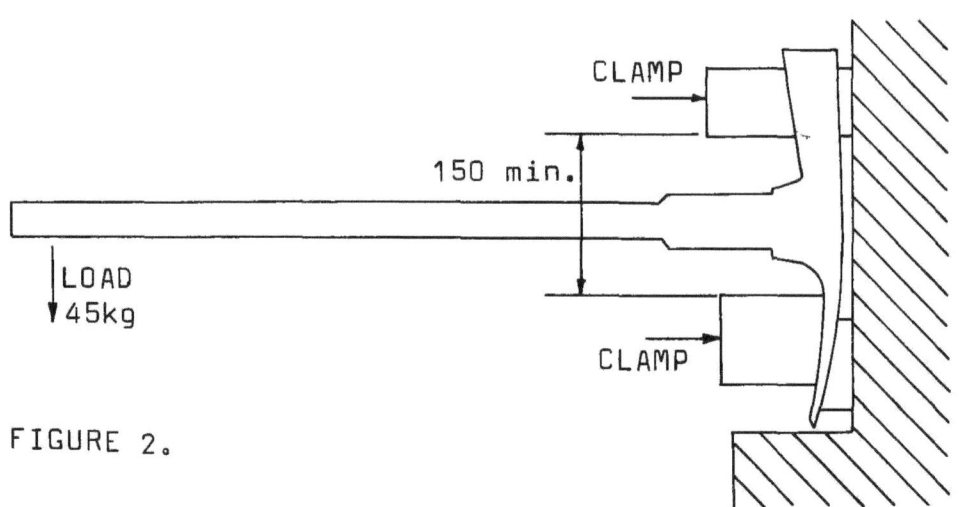

FIGURE 2.

SPECIFICATION No. 113 — SHOVEL HANDLE

Material

Hardwood seasoned to not more than 20% moisture content.

Testing

With the plain end of the handle firmly clamped over a length of 150mm a load of 45 kilograms shall be gradually applied by suspension at the grip, with an offset from the handle centreline of 150mm. (This can be achieved conveniently by sliding a well-fitting tube over the 35mm grip diameter.)

There must be no failure, cracking, or permanent set in excess of 25mm on removal of the load.

Samples

Any supplier must submit three samples for dimensional, material, and strength approval, before proceeding with production.

Marking

Handles to be stamped 113 in bold figures.

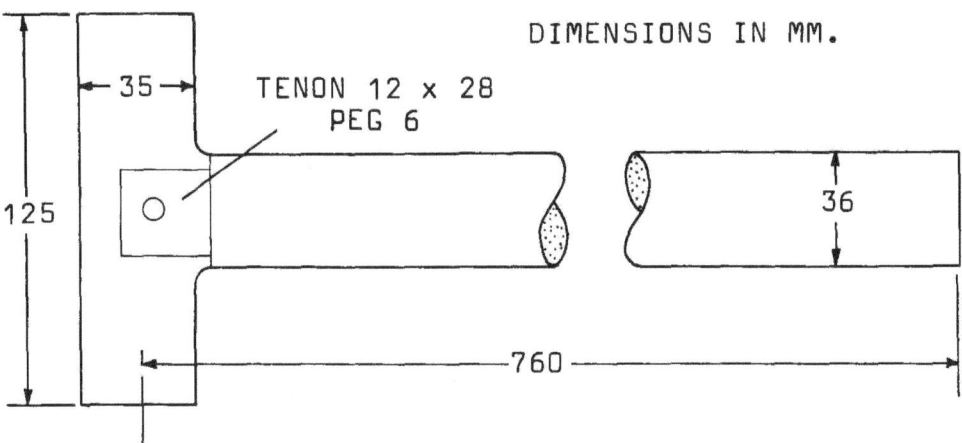

DIMENSIONS IN MM.

SPECIFICATION No. 114A — JEMBE/FORK JEMBE HANDLE

Material

Hardwood seasoned to not more than 20% moisture content.

Testing

With the larger end clamped over a length of 120mm a load of 45 kilograms shall be gradually applied by suspension at the free end of the handle. There must be no failure, cracking, or permanent set in excess of 25mm on removal of the load.

Samples

Any supplier must submit three samples for dimensional, material, and strength approval, before proceeding with production.

Marking

Handles to be stamped 114A in bold figures.

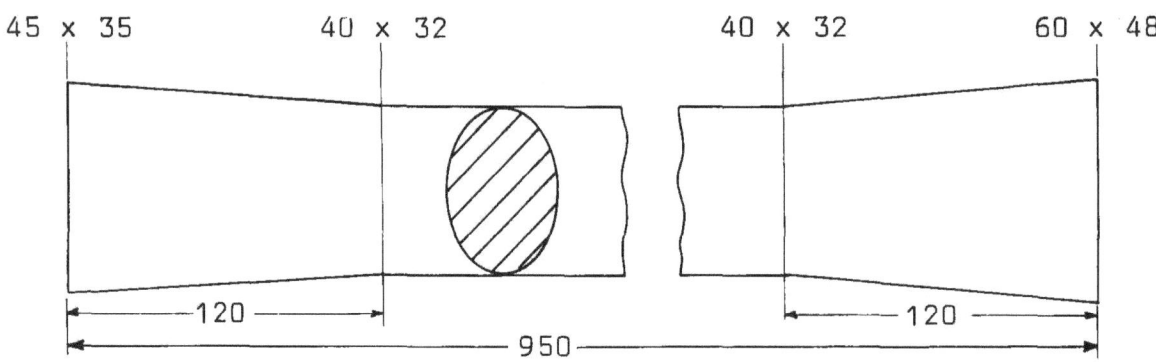

SPECIFICATION No. 114B — PICK/MATTOCK HANDLE

Material

Hardwood seasoned to not more than 20% moisture content.

Testing

With the larger end clamped over a length of 120mm a load of 45 kilograms shall be gradually applied by suspension at the free end of the handle. There must be no failure, cracking, or permanent set in excess of 25mm on removal of the load.

Samples

Any supplier must submit three samples for dimensional, material, and strength approval, before proceeding with production.

Marking

Handles to be stamped 114B in bold figures.

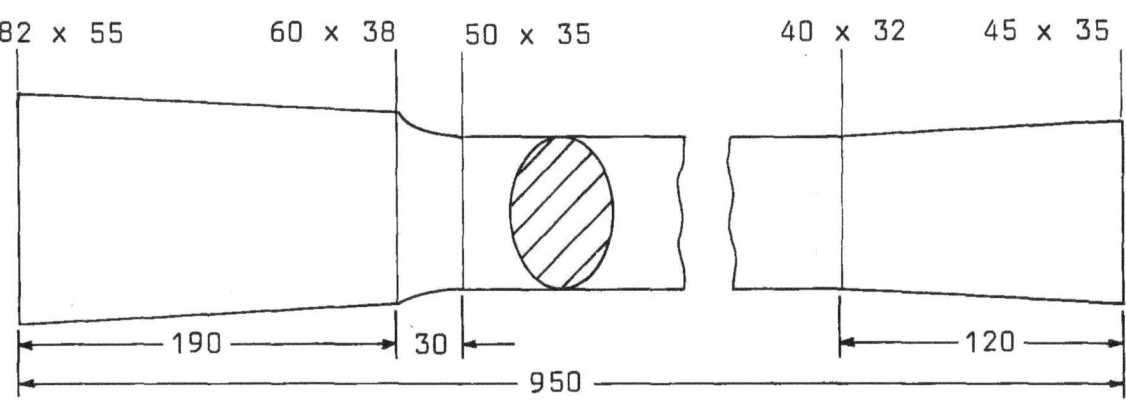

SPECIFICATION No. 114C — AXE HANDLE

Material

Hardwood seasoned to not more than 20% moisture content.

Testing

With the larger end clamped over a length of 100mm a load of 45 kilograms shall be gradually applied by suspension at the free end of the handle, and maintained for two minutes. There must be no failure, cracking, or permanent set in excess of 25mm on removal of the load.

Samples

Any supplier must submit three samples for dimensional, material, and strength approval, before proceeding with production.

Marking

Handles to be stamped in bold figures 114C at the handgrip end.

DIMENSIONS IN MM.

69 x 26   60 x 32   40 x 32   40 x 32   45 x 35
          72 x 30

100 — 25 — 50 — 150 — 120

920

SPECIFICATION No. 114E — SLEDGEHAMMER HANDLE

Material

Hardwood free from defects seasoned to not more than 20% moisture content.

Testing

With the hammer end clamped over a length of 150mm a load of 40 kilograms shall be gradually applied by suspension at the free end of the handle. There must be no failure, cracking, or permanent set in excess of 10mm on removal of the load.

Samples

Any supplier must submit three samples for dimensional, material, and strength approval, before proceeding with production.

Marking

Handles to be stamped in bold figures 114E at the handgrip end.

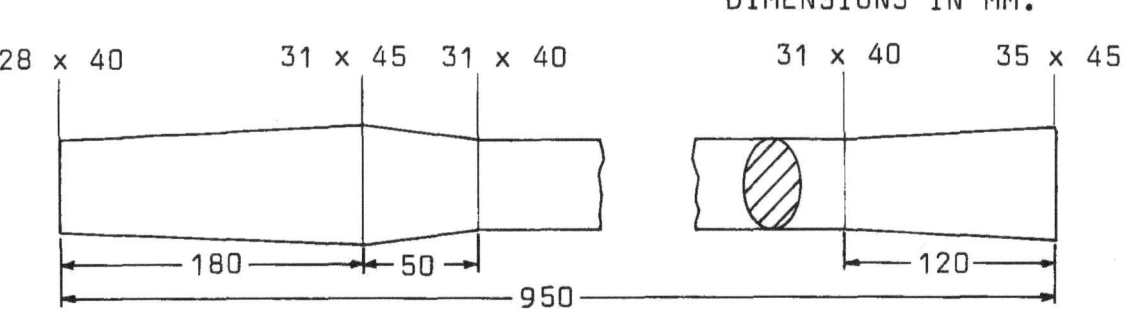

SPECIFICATION No. 115 — AXE

Note: For an axe to be effective and retain its edge a high grade chrome manganese steel must be used. It must be forged and heat treated. In general this means that axes have to be imported. The fitting of the handles is a specialised operation.

Weight
2.3 kilograms (+10%, −5%).

Material Specification (Steel)

Carbon	Manganese	Chromium	Silicon	Phosphorus	Sulphur
Percent	*Percent*	*Percent*	*Percent*	*Percent*	*Percent*
0.55 min	0.80 max	0.45 min	0.35 max	0.06 max	0.06 max

Heat Treatment and Hardness
The forging shall be hardened and tempered to produce Rockwell C 25/30 at the eye, increasing to Rockwell C 48/54 within 50mm of the cutting edge.

Construction
The forging must be symmetrical and free from flaws. All fins and flashes must be dressed off. The eye must be smooth internally, uniformly tapered, and must lie central within 0.5mm in the forging. The cutting edge must be ground sharp.

Fitting of the Handles
Handles (to specification No.114C) may be fitted by means of softwood wedges or by chemical adhesive bonding.

Testing
a. With a standard hardwood handle fitted and the tool clamped as shown on Figure 2 a load of 45kg shall be gradually applied by suspension at the end of the handle and maintained for two minutes. On removal of the load the tool shall show no signs of damage to the head or loosening of the handle, nor shall there be any permanent set in excess of 25mm measured at the handle end.
b. The head/handle joint shall withstand an end load of 500kg without loosening.
c. The tool shall withstand a minimum of twenty very heavy blows across the grain of a hardwood without damage to the cutting edge or loosening of the handle.

Marking
The forging shall be clearly and indelibly marked with the following:
a. Manufacturer's name and/or trademark.
b. The figures 115.
c. The nominal weight.

Preservative Treatment
The head shall be bright finished all over and varnished.

SPECIFICATION No.115 DIMENSIONS IN MM.

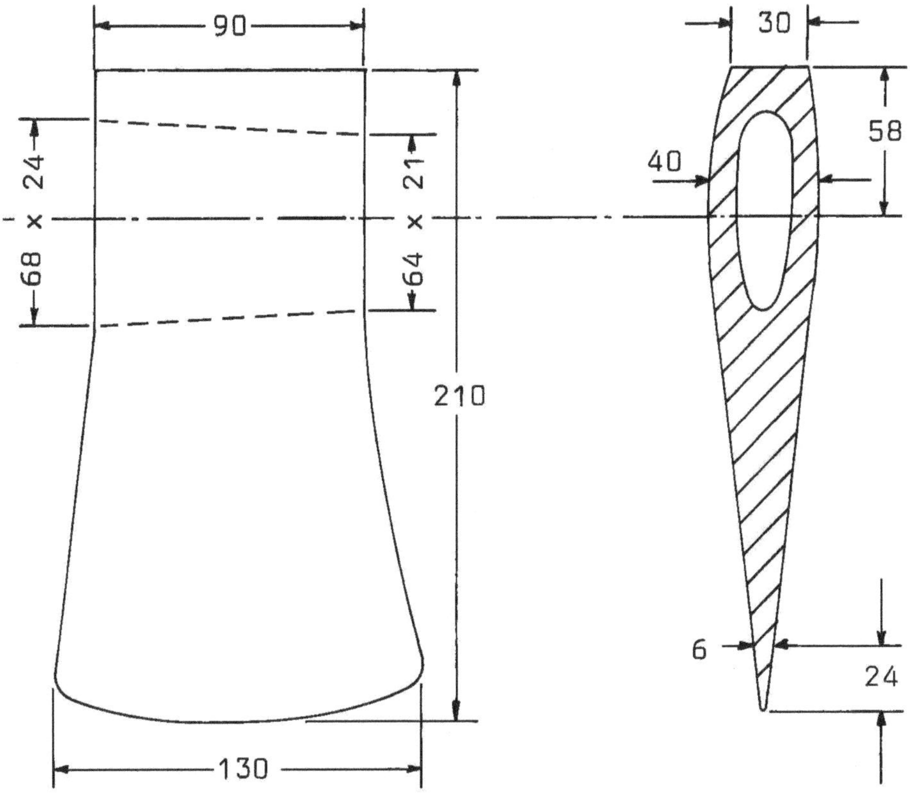

FIGURE 1

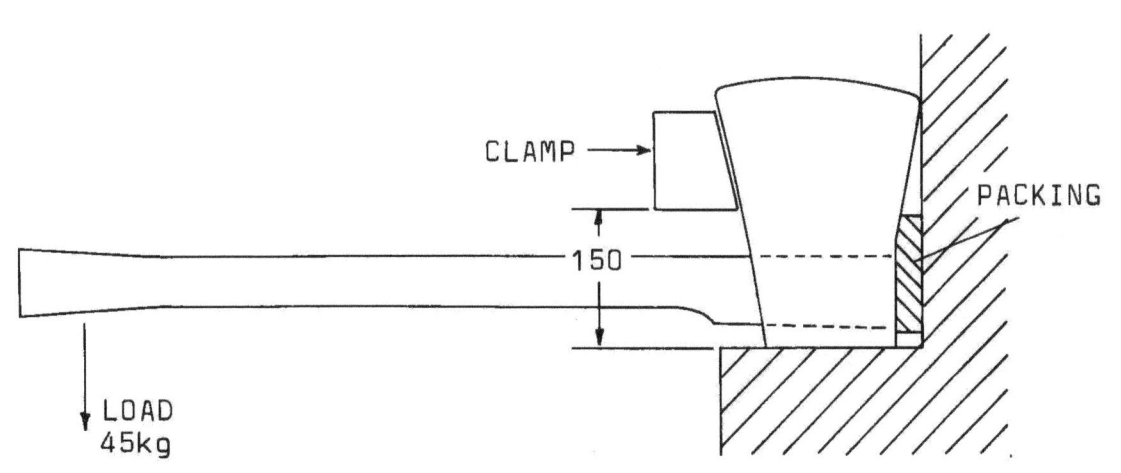

FIGURE 2.

SPECIFICATION No. 116 — PICKAXE

Note: It is essential that pickaxes be forged from the medium carbon steel specified and heat-treated as indicated.

Weight

3.2kg (+10%, −5%).

Material Specification (Steel)

Carbon *Percent*	Manganese *Percent*	Phosphorus *Percent*	Sulphur *Percent*
0.40/0.50	0.50/0.80	0.05 max	0.05 max

Heat Treatment and Hardness

The forging shall be hardened and tempered to produce Rockwell C 25/30 at the eye, increasing to Rockwell C45/50 within 50mm of the cutting edges.

Construction

The forging must be symmetrical and free from flaws. All fins and flashes must be dressed off. The eye must be smooth internally, uniformly tapered, and must lie centrally in the forging.

The thickness of the blades shall be greatest at the shoulders, decreasing towards the cutting edge and point, which must be ground sharp.

Testing

With a standard hardwood handle fitted and the tool clamped as shown on Figure 2 a load of 45kg shall be gradually applied by suspension at the end of the handle and maintained for two minutes. On removal of the load the tool shall show no signs of damage to the head or loosening of the handle, nor shall there be any permanent set in excess of 25mm measured at the handle end.

The cutting edge and point shall be struck a sharp blow with a bar of mild steel 25mm diameter. No fracture or deformation must occur.

Marking

The forging shall be clearly and indelibly marked with the following:

a. Manufacturer's name and/or trademark.

b. The figures 116.

c. The nominal weight.

Preservative Treatment

The head to be varnished all over.

SPECIFICATION No.116　　　　　　　DIMENSIONS IN MM.

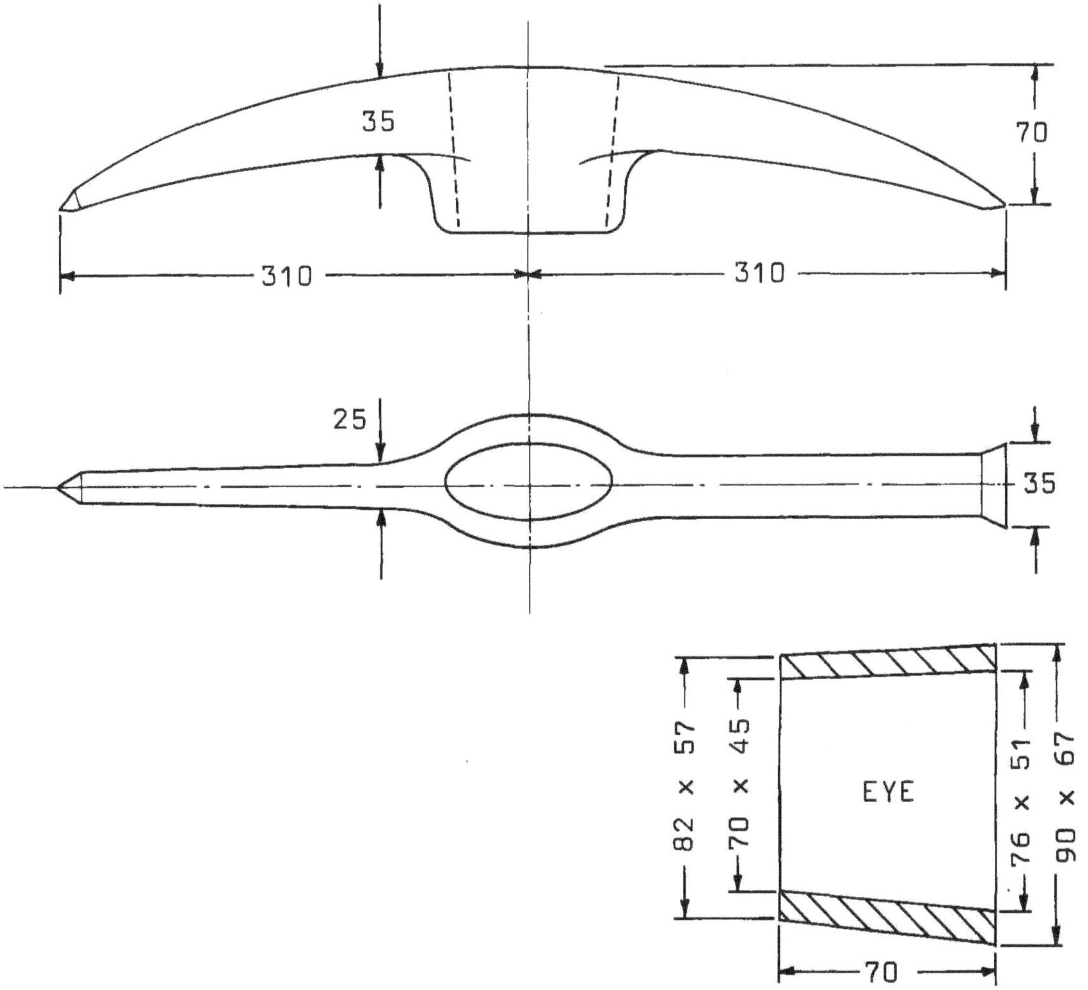

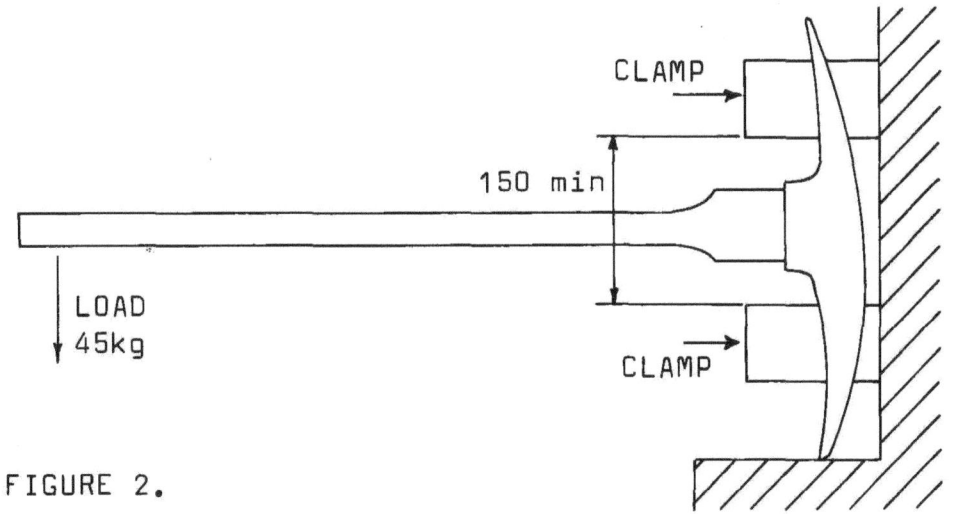

FIGURE 1.

FIGURE 2.

SPECIFICATION No. 117 — SPREADER

Note: Garden rakes or up-graded versions of them are not satisfactory under arduous field conditions. This is a simple but appropriate tool.

Weight
3kg nominal.

Material
Steel. Blade to have carbon content 0.20/0.30 per cent.
Handle to be hardwood 1500mm long.

Construction
Socket and braces to be welded or riveted to blade.

Treatment
Paint all over with preservative paint.

Marking
The Spreader to be clearly and indelibly marked with:

a. Manufacturers name and/or trademark.

b. The figures 117

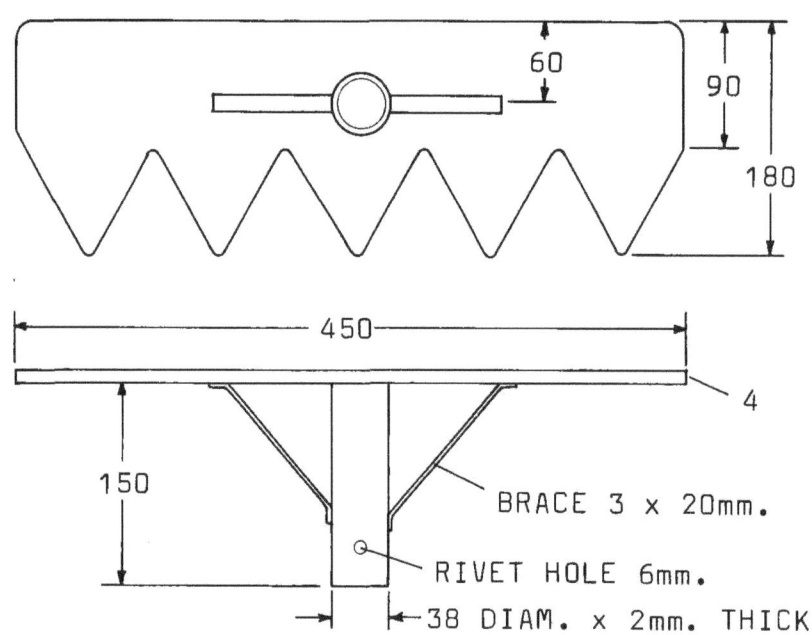

NOTE: HANDLE TO BE HARDWOOD 1500mm. LONG

SPECIFICATION No. 118 — RAMMER

A simple but appropriate tool that is easy to make and useful in service.

Weight
8kg nominal.

Material
Steel. Canister 100mm diameter with material thickness 3mm minimum. End discs 6mm thick. Socket thickness 2mm minimum.
Handle to be seasoned hardwood 1100mm long.

Construction
Weld bottom disc to canister. Fill with sand. Weld on top disc. Weld socket and braces to top disc. (Note: Canister can be made from pipe or rolled up and seam welded sheet.)

Treatment
Paint all over with preservative paint.

Marking
The Rammer to be clearly and indelibly marked with:

a. Manufacturer's name and/or trademark.

b. The figures 118.

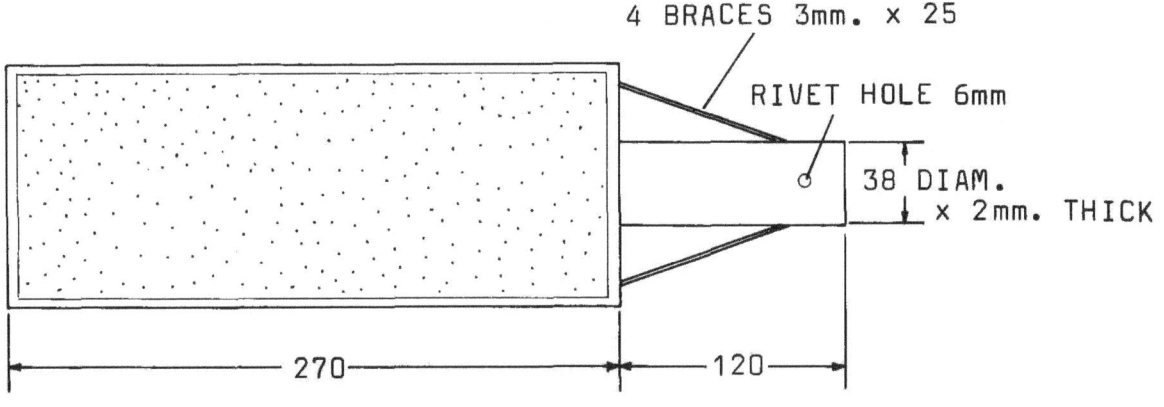

NOTE: HANDLE TO BE HARDWOOD 1100mm. LONG

'This book leads the reader through metaphor, wonder and play to a deeper appreciation of science and God. If you have wondered how science and religious faith can be held together, this book is for you.'

**Dr Bethany Sollereder, lecturer in science and religion,
The University of Edinburgh**

'This is a book of profound pictures – stunning images of the cosmos coupled with pictures of the wonder and playfulness of being both a scientist and a Christian. David Gregory explodes the myth that science and faith are boring! Rather he stimulates the imagination and engages curiosity to get to a picture of God that is compelling and liberating.'

David Wilkinson, professor of theology and religion, Durham University

'David Gregory doesn't just argue that science and faith can coexist – he shows us how science can become a sacred lens through which we glimpse the presence of God. As a filmmaker, I believe in the power of image, beauty and story to open hearts and reawaken the imagination. This book does exactly that. It invites the people to rediscover a deeper vision of Christ – not just as the Lord of Sunday mornings, but as the one in whom stars burn, tectonic plates shift and every breath holds divine mystery. This is not just a helpful book. It's a needed one.'

The Revd Andy Thomas, Baptist pioneer minister, producer and director, Fuelcast Films

'This is a wonderful book that truly opens divine windows. David Gregory moves effortlessly between science and faith with an easy style that gives the reader confidence to explore these vast topics together. David explores the way art and science interweave and stimulate our imagination to see new horizons. Prepare to be inspired!'
**The Revd Margot R. Hodson, director of theology and education,
The John Ray Initiative**

'Here is an affirmation of the visual and of imagination, awe and wonder in both science and theology… We are given a deep groundwork as preparation for spiritual reflection on scientific images, before being let loose to explore some pictures from astronomy for ourselves, with enough scientific and theological content to fire the imagination. This is a beautiful book to give to thinking friends, family and colleagues, as well as a resource for the church.'
Dr Ruth M. Bancewicz, church engagement director, The Faraday Institute for Science and Religion

This book is delightfully full of the familiar and the unfamiliar. Incredible images and arresting turns of phrase are brought together to give fresh perspectives around the intermingling of science, theology and the arts. It is most worthy of your time, your attention… and your spirit. Take up its invitation to dwell in all the richness and beauty that being a creature alive in God's creation involves today!'
Dr Gavin Merrifield, general secretary of Christians in Science

'Using his studies and experience of both science and theology David Gregory gives useful reflections to aid the praise and worship of our creator and the creator of the whole cosmos. David helpfully encourages us to use our imagination and powers of observation in discovering the infinite love of the creator, the creator's genius and invention displayed through design and ever fresh novelty and originality, wisdom, order and playfulness of creation… I believe that this book will help many in their contemplation and worship.'
The Revd Dr John Weaver, former principle of Cardiff Baptist College and vice president of The John Ray Initiative

'We have all got caught up in science versus religion as an idea we have to live with "and it has blinkered us." What David Gregory through *Divine Windows* aims to do is to move into plain view the narrative imagination from which most of the scientific method actually emerges – and therefore create a space where this whole, stagnant debate can be reframed. David believes that this is an unexplored territory and through reframing we will be able to see the fingerprints of God and that will lead to human flourishing.'
Michael Harvey, missional entrepreneur, director 'God and the Big Bang'

'This book is written in a very accessible and engaging style. But the reader should not be fooled – this is a book full of ingenuity and subtlety of thought, shedding fresh light on familiar debates and opening up telling visual imagery to offer the explorer paths into a deeper appreciation of the wonder of God's cosmos. Warmly recommended!'
Professor Christopher Southgate, University of Exeter

 Ministries

15 The Chambers, Vineyard
Abingdon OX14 3FE
+44 (0)1865 319700 | brf.org.uk

Bible Reading Fellowship (BRF) is a charity (233280)
and company limited by guarantee (301324),
registered in England and Wales

EU Authorised Representative: Easy Access System Europe –
Mustamäe tee 50, 10621 Tallinn, Estonia, **gpsr.requests@easproject.com**

ISBN 978 1 80039 331 8
First published 2025
10 9 8 7 6 5 4 3 2 1 0
All rights reserved

Text © David Gregory 2025
This edition © Bible Reading Fellowship 2025
Cover and inside images © National Aeronautics and Space Administration (NASA)

The author asserts the moral right to be identified as the author of this work

Acknowledgements

Unless otherwise acknowledged, scripture quotations are taken from The Holy Bible, New International Version (Anglicised edition) copyright © 1979, 1984, 2011 by Biblica. Used by permission of Hodder & Stoughton Publishers, a Hachette UK company. All rights reserved. 'NIV' is a registered trademark of Biblica. UK trademark number 1448790. Quotations marked NRSV are taken from The New Revised Standard Version, Updated Edition. Copyright © 2021 National Council of Churches of Christ in the United States of America. Used by permission. All rights reserved worldwide.

Every effort has been made to trace and contact copyright owners for material used in this resource. We apologise for any inadvertent omissions or errors, and would ask those concerned to contact us so that full acknowledgement can be made in the future.

A catalogue record for this book is available from the British Library

Printed and bound in the UK by Zenith Media NP4 0DQ

David Gregory

DIVINE WINDOWS

—

Seeing God through
the lens of science

Contents

1. A pilgrimage in science and faith 9
2. Clearing the view 21
3. Art, science and God 37
4. Exercising the imagination 49
5. The stuff of science and God: wonder, playfulness and order 61
6. Divine windows 83
   - Star 87
   - Moon 93
   - Earth 97
   - Aurora 103
   - Dust 107
   - Life 113
   - Other worlds 121
   - Cosmos 127

Epilogue: gazing with God 133

Notes 137

1

A pilgrimage in science and faith

Postcards from Coventry

Coventry is a city in the heart of England with a long history, from the medieval era through the Industrial Revolution to the present day. Much of its industrial heritage has now faded, as has its historic medieval centre, lost in the bombing of World War II. The Medieval Guild Hall survived; the old Cathedral Church of St Michael's lies in ruins. Next to it stands the new, modern St Michael's Cathedral, renowned not only for its architecture but for its focus and work on reconciliation and peace building.

Attracted by its architectural design and stunning windows, along with spiritual motivations, over 100,000 people visit the new cathedral each year.

Yet the phrase 'being sent to Coventry' has darker tones. As with many old English sayings, its origin lies hidden in the mists of time. It might have originated during the English Civil War of the 17th century between King Charles I and Parliament. At that time, Coventry housed Royalist prisoners, but they were not well received by the Parliament-supporting population. Through the years 'being sent to Coventry' has come to mean a person being sidelined by their family, work colleagues or wider community – a lonely and hurtful experience to endure.

I'm glad to say that I have never been 'sent to Coventry'. But I have been to the city three times, and on each occasion I have visited the cathedrals. Each visit has also involved science.

On the first occasion, in my late teens, I attended a science taster day at the university. In the physics lab, we exposed old pre-decimal silver sixpences to a radioactive source, measuring the time it took for the radiation absorbed by the coins to decay. From this, we could measure how much true 'silver' was in the coins, so dating when cheaper metals began to be included. From 1920, following World War I, the amount of silver was gradually reduced. After World War II, in 1947, 'silver' coins contained no silver at all.

While the purpose of this first trip was to experience what studying science at university might be like, there was also time to visit the nearby cathedrals. The old standing next to the new is a symbol of the hope of reconciliation in a broken world, of which being sent to Coventry is a part. I don't recall much of my impression from that visit. Certainly, there was no religious motivation or moment of spiritual encounter. While I chose to go to Coventry rather than being sent there, it was a time in my life when you might say that I had sent God to Coventry. Growing up within a church community, my growing interest in science led me to walk away from the Christian faith and belief in God. Within the rational view of the world, there seemed to be no space for such a being or need of such belief.

I next visited Coventry over 30 years later. This time, both science and faith were part of the experience. I was attending an evening event at the cathedral with distinguished speakers from the world of science, sharing their perspectives on how the two areas of human thought and experience might be held together. The cathedral was packed with people of all ages. For some, faith was a part of their lives. Many were students from local universities who, like me at that stage of life, had already sent or were thinking of sending God to Coventry. The resulting questions and debate were varied and rigorous, but in keeping with the spirit of reconciliation that is at the heart of the work of the cathedral, the atmosphere was generous.

Much had changed in my life in the years between these visits. I had studied science at university and worked for over a decade for the Met Office and the European Centre for Medium-Range Weather Forecasts, developing weather and climate models. While my love and passion for scientific exploration remained, out of it had arisen a journey of faith that eventually led me to become a church minister. After 20 years in that role, my journey in life was beginning to take a new direction that wove together both narratives.

My third visit to the cathedral, a few years later, also involved the connection between science and faith. This time, I was not in the audience but part of a team from 'God and the Big Bang'. I had moved away from serving as a minister of a local church to focus on helping people in church and beyond to explore issues around science and faith. On this occasion, we were working with over a hundred 15- and 16-year-olds from local schools, only a few years younger than the age at which I first visited the cathedral.

While the students that day came from local schools with church connections, they were of many different faiths and none. Like me at their age, many of them came having already sent God to Coventry. Throughout the day, there were sessions on topics such as the Big Bang, evolution and climate change. We explored how science and faith view the world and life, together with their connections and seeming conflicts.

At the end of the day, questions were invited from the young people on science and faith. They were thought-provoking and at times stretched and developed the team's ideas of how science and faith can both be a part of their lives. At times we had to say, 'We don't know.' This statement, important in both science and faith, acknowledges there is more to explore and experience as we seek understanding of the world and our place within in. For in both areas, questions are important, more so than the certainty of truths.

Sent to Coventry

This sense of openness may be a surprise to many. The widely held belief is that the certainty of science's description and understanding of the world has sent God to Coventry. Over 50 years ago, at the end of the 1960s, the sociologist Peter Berger lamented that for most people, including many of the young people visiting Coventry Cathedral that day, 'the supernatural as a meaningful reality is absent or remote from the horizons of everyday life'.[1]

Through the half-century since Berger's reflection, the gift of science has continued to shape and enhance human life in many ways. The development of the internet and worldwide web has made communication with people around the world an everyday experience. Understanding our genetic make-up is leading to new medical treatments and helped stem the effects of the Covid-19 pandemic with the rapid development of effective vaccines. While we continue to complain about the accuracy of weather forecasts, with vast amounts of data provided by satellites continually orbiting the Earth, their accuracy has improved remarkably – honest!

Many people also find science puzzling and overwhelming. There is a growing distrust of science, for example, in the anxiety over artificial intelligence or where genetic engineering may take the human species. Yet at the same time, there is an appetite for popular presentations of science. Science stories regularly appear on mainstream news programmes and social media feeds. Science and natural history series attract huge audiences, their stunning imagery evoking a sense of awe and wonder. It is an experience that leaves viewers drawn beyond everyday experience, leading them towards a transcendent, spiritual realm. Yet so often these popular programmes paint a picture of a world where God has been sent to Coventry.

Within the worship of the Christian community, such imagery also increasingly appears. Yet, perhaps here too, there has been a failure to appreciate the value of this scientific imagery for facilitating divine encounter. Might it provide a fresh way of inviting people to encounter God?

Returning from Coventry

Popular science and nature presentations are nothing new. In medieval western Europe, 'bestiaries' were popular. Lavishly illustrated books, akin to nature documentaries today, they described diverse types of animals, both real and mythical. They were a celebration of God's creativity and wisdom in creation, evoking curiosity and praise.

Further back still, the script of the first science and nature programme can be found in the Bible. The book of Job tells the story of a man who endures tragedy, loss and pain that rob him of fullness of life. He cries out to God, seeking understanding. Friends gather around him and through many words seek to help him find answers to his questions and complaints. At the end of the story, God turns up in person, not with more words, nor with answers, but inviting Job to look at the wonders of creation: up to the clouds and stars, around at the habitats and habits of a wide variety of animals, and down into the depths of the sea. At the end of it all, Job puts his questions to one side and declares: 'My ears had heard of you but now my eyes have seen you' (Job 42:5). For Job, seeing the wonder of creation means that God is brought back from Coventry.

In an age when we glimpse the wonders of nature and the cosmos in a deeper and wider way than earlier generations, how, like Job, can people's view of the world be awakened to see the divine presence through science's vision? Or as Timothy Radcliffe, the former head of the Roman Catholic Dominican order, asks, 'How can Christianity reawaken the imagination of our contemporaries?'[2]

Certainly, on my third visit to Coventry Cathedral, my imagination was stirred. Looking around the cathedral buildings, they spoke to me about science and faith. Like the cathedrals of old, there are wondrous stained-glass windows. Some are more abstract than others, yet they still have the ability to speak. The floor-to-ceiling curved Baptistery Window, which contains nearly 200 brightly coloured glass panels, fills the interior with rainbow coloured light. The rainbow is a natural wonder which has captivated people through the ages, created by the chance interplay of the powerful, ancient Sun and fragile, momentary raindrops. The distinct colours of light bend at slightly different angles as they pass through the raindrop, smearing an arc of colour across the sky. Power and fragility combine, becoming a symbol of hope, for the Bible speaks of the rainbow being placed in the sky by God as a sign of divine care for all living things.

In Coventry Cathedral, rainbow light dances over the font, carved in the form of a scallop shell into a boulder from Bethlehem, the birthplace of Jesus. This ancient symbol, carried by pilgrims, is an appropriate choice to mark the beginning of the Christian journey in baptism. And over the polished, stone floor of the cathedral, the rainbow light continues to spill and shimmer.

This floor marks the pilgrimage of life through millions of years revealed by science. Looking down as you walk along the cathedral's central aisle towards the altar, perhaps missed by many visitors whose vision is drawn up to the magnificence of the openness of the space, you walk on a carpet of fossilised shells. A memory of a world and life long since vanished, the carpet of shells marks the rich playfulness of evolution's game which has shaped life through the long history of the Earth. Sea creatures who basked in the flickering light of the Sun in shallow seas are now caressed by rainbow light, recalling God's creativity expressed within the natural world, which the divine artist declared as 'very good' in the Bible's creation story.

Good, wondrous and yet fragile. Over millions of years, competition for food and habitats, random changes in genetic code, cosmic events like the asteroid strike that contributed to the extinction of the dinosaurs, together with slow shifts in the Earth's climate, led to the passing of such life beneath my feet. A fluid moment within the long history of the Earth is now immortalised in beautiful solidity. New forms have dynamically arisen to take their place, a sign of the continuing creativity of God.

Yet, what of the suffering and death ever present from the beginning of the world? This is an ancient question arising from human experience, now asked in a wider way as science has revealed the twists and turns of the long journey of the Earth through the past four-and-a-half billion years. It causes us to question God's care for the world and for ourselves in our pilgrimage of life. These questions have been asked through millennia, with answers being hard to find.

Watching over you as you walk across this carpet of wonder and tears is a huge tapestry of 'Christ in Glory', Lord of all creation – the one, as John's gospel says, through whom all things were made: the risen, ascended Lord Jesus, alive yet still bearing the marks of death, of nails in his hand and feet, eternal symbols of Christ's bearing the brokenness of the world on the cross at Easter. He sustains the hope of life in the face of the continual suffering, for 'through him [God reconciles] to himself all things, whether things on earth or things in heaven, by making peace through his blood, shed on the cross' (Colossians 1:20). As with Job, this is not a definitive answer. Where science and faith embrace, there is the need to say, 'I don't know!' Still, in our unknowing, hope can be seen.

Signals of transcendence

Those who designed and decorated Coventry Cathedral with such signs and symbols perhaps never intended to speak to the relationship and reconciliation of science and faith. Yet, that is the power of signs and symbols.

They have a fluidity, revealing new layers of meaning to the viewer. Truth is revealed not through the lens of the rational and technical, but through a playful, imaginative lens.

While Peter Berger lamented the loss of a sense of divine presence within people's vision of the world, he was not without hope that their imagination could be reawakened. He saw in people's everyday experience 'signals of transcendence'[13] pointing beyond material reality. Among them are the activity of play and the search for order within life, along with wonder, which the imagery of science so often evokes. Rather than science's vision sending God to Coventry, perhaps through what it shows of the world it may reveal such 'signals of transcendence', allowing people to journey further through the scientific vision of the world towards divine encounter.

This is the possibility that this book explores. Later, in chapter 6, we will look at some of the amazing images of the Earth, Solar System and cosmos that spacecraft and telescopes have given us over the past 60 years. But before we arrive there, we need to train our eyes to look differently through science's vision of the material world and cosmos. We may need to be fitted for a new pair of glasses that will soften the seeming solidity of what science reveals about the world and universe, enabling a fluid, imaginative view – akin to how the work of human art is viewed – that reveals meaning through signs and symbols rather than material descriptions, concepts and processes.

On this pilgrimage, we begin looking at the role visual experience plays within the Bible and the history of faith. Drawing upon the experience of Orthodox and western Christianity's use of art to facilitate prayer, together with Franciscan insights into how God might be glimpsed within creation, we will explore how imagery leads to spiritual encounter and awareness of the transcendent. Imagination plays a huge part in this, so we will need to look at the role it plays in theology, art and science. Then bringing all these strands together, we will shape lenses to gaze on the imagery of science based on Berger's themes of wonder, playfulness and order – themes which shape the process of science itself – bringing into focus the divine presence in science's vision. Finally, with our new spectacles, we will gaze upon some of the wondrous images of the cosmos that science provides.

So, come and join the journey, looking at the wonder of creation and for the wonder of the creator!

Clearing the view

A night at the museum

A Night at the Museum is a children's book written by Milan Trenc, later made into a film set in the American Museum of Natural History in New York. The museum's new nightwatchman is surprised to find that the exhibits – from dinosaurs to wild animals and a gum-chewing Easter Island statue – come to life every night, causing havoc! Its success led to two sequels, the final one involving a trip to the British Museum in London, with similar chaos ensuing as Egyptian mummies come back to life. Building on the success of the films, the British Museum, along with others, organise all-night events for groups of children to have a sleepover among the exhibits.

My night at the British Museum was not as wild or exciting, but it was memorable and significant. The museum houses some renowned artifacts documenting human culture across the millennia and world. It's a favourite place for my wife and I to spend time in when we travel down to London, wandering among the regular exhibits as well as special displays. A few years ago, we spent the evening visiting the 'Living with the Gods'[4] exhibit. Through sacred and ordinary objects, it imaginatively wove the story of humanity's exploration of the transcendent and faith, from 40,000 years ago during the last Ice Age to the late 20th century. Two objects, from the end and beginning of the exhibit, caught my attention, speaking of the intersection of art, science and faith.

First, near the end of the exhibit, a poster from the USSR epitomised the idea that science had sent God to Coventry – or whatever the Russian equivalent is! Celebrating the first human space flight in 1961, it showed an orange-space-suited Yuri Gagarin outside of his spacecraft, Vostok 1, both floating above the domes and steeples of Russian Orthodox churches, such as those of St Basil's Cathedral lying next to the fortress of the Kremlin in Moscow's Red Square. A caption confidently declares 'БОГА НЕТ!' – 'There is no God!' This propaganda proclaimed the official atheistic position of the Soviet government and the triumph of technological science over faith.

Second, in contrast, an object near the start of the exhibit suggested the possibility of a different conversation between science and faith. It was a statue of the four-armed Hindu god Shiva as Nataraja – Lord of the Dance. Alongside this small object was a picture of a larger version, not set within a Hindu temple, as you might expect, but in the grounds of CERN near Geneva, the home of the Large Hadron Collider, which is currently the largest particle accelerator in the world, 27 kilometres around.

The statue depicts the cycle of creation and destruction of the cosmos within the Hindu world view. With one hand, Shiva plays a drum, to the rhythm of which he dances, so creating the world. In another, he holds fire, symbolic of its destruction. The caption underneath the statue describes it as a gift from the Indian government, marking the collaboration of Indian and European scientists. It was chosen because it expresses resonance between the cosmic dance of Nataraja and the continual interchange of energy and matter, the creation and destruction of subatomic particles, seen at the smallest scales of the universe. Imaginatively, this statue brings scientific and faith perspectives together, the spiritual being glimpsed through the material.

Different ways of seeing

In an age when science is so often assumed to have sent God to Coventry, the sociologist Peter Berger suggests that communities who continue to hold to belief in God can suffer 'cognitive dissonance'. Negotiating a culture in which science is accepted as the dominant story, at both individual and societal levels, can result in anxiety and bewilderment. This clash of perspectives, Berger suggests, leads to a triad of responses: surrender, defiance and bargaining.[5]

Surrender, at the extreme, is captured by the Soviet poster proclaiming there is no God. Traditional stories of faith are de-mythologised or the sense of divine action removed, such as explaining miracles in terms of natural phenomena that are or might be in the future explained scientifically. It strips religious belief down to a set of moral imperatives aimed at helping people to live well.

Alternatively, surrender might be characterised by separation: an acceptance of science's perspectives on the world, while holding to traditional expressions and understandings of faith and sacred texts, yet with little interaction between the two. While enjoying the benefits of science and technology within everyday life, there is a failure to reflect upon what science might mean for understandings of faith. In many churches, science as a subject is rarely if ever broached in sermons and discussions. Those involved in the world of science are left at the back, looking after the AV and PA equipment. This is a scenario which hides and fails to address a sense of cognitive dissonance they and other members of faith communities may feel, leaving them living in two different worlds, the sacred and the secular, ill-prepared to engage with wider world views.

Defiance too might leave people similarly ill-equipped. Characteristic of streams of the church with a strong focus upon biblical literalism, traditional faith perspectives are valued above scientific perspectives in defining how the world and cosmos should be seen. This is an inversion of the position depicted by the Soviet poster, in which God reigns triumphant over science.

Positively, defiance flows from a desire to be faithful to divine revelation in Jesus and the Bible. On the flip side, it can also flow from anxiety and fear; of the consequences of failing to be faithful to tradition and divine command, but also over whether the faith of individuals and community can withstand the force of science's vision – another form of surrender. Significant issues on which science speaks, such as the consequences of human-caused climate change or the value of vaccines, can be discounted or actively resisted. Members of faith communities are led to a distrust of science, finding themselves living between two worlds: the seeming security of the world of faith and the insecurity and danger of the views of the wider culture.

A conversation with some young people in a school I visited several years ago highlighted for me a possible consequence of defiance. I was invited to talk about the science of climate change to a group of students. Organised by the science department, connections between science and faith were not part of the brief. But, introducing myself as a minister with a background in science led to a question from one of the students: 'How can you be a scientist and a Christian? You have to believe in evolution if you're a scientist.'

After the session, the questioner approached me again, this time with a group of their friends. I discovered they all attended the same local church, and I asked them: 'Does your church teach you that if you are a Christian you have to believe what the Bible says about how the Earth and life came to be?' 'Yes' was their reply. Two things concerned me about this conversation. Firstly, the danger that this group of young people are not equipped by their faith leaders to hold together science and faith. And, secondly, when they encounter a bigger world beyond school and church, through music and media, mixing with people with different perspectives in social and work settings, will they have the ability, resilience and imaginative flexibility for faith to be sustained and renegotiated?

Where science and faith are engaged within Christian communities, it is often around apologetics. Relying on rational ideas and arguments, it holds open the reasonableness of faith and the possibility of the supernatural in the face of the success and seeming certainty of the science. It invites people to consider issues where science and faith overlap, such as understanding the origin of the universe and life, questions around miracles and how God might be understood as acting within science's view of the world.

This rational approach can play a positive role within a defiant stance, though there can be the temptation to undermine science and elevate faith views. Example of 'defiant apologetics' might include creationism and creation science which take a more literal view of the biblical creation narratives, although some creation-science approaches tend towards bargaining.

Lying between surrender and defiance, **bargaining** involves a reshaping of some faith traditions while others are kept. Generally, scientific views are more accepted, yet the possibility of God acting through and beyond science is retained. For example, evolution is accommodated alongside a view that sees God as the creator of life, working gradually through the evolutionary process or nudging it to fulfil divine purpose. Apologetics can play a positive role in this bargaining. However, such accommodation can raise some significant questions. Within evolution, suffering and death are endemic features of the pilgrimage of life from its earliest times, in contrast to traditional Christian perspectives that the 'fallenness' of the world stems from human disobedience to God's commands.

A brief history of seeing God

While apologetic approaches have proved useful in keeping the story of God alive in a scientific age, their weakness is that they appeal solely to reason and neglect the human imagination. Apologetic approaches play science at its own game. They draw upon the same 'technocratic imagination' that is at the heart of the scientific approach to the world that has flourished since the 18th century. In his book *A Secular Age*, the philosopher Charles Taylor characterised this approach as a way of gaining knowledge, in both fields of science and faith, through rational examination of 'scripture; or… what [God] has made'. Based around concepts and mechanism, it leads to a 'disenchantment'[6] of the world – in other words, sending God to Coventry.

Taylor dates the rise of the technocratic approach to long before the scientific age of the past few centuries – back to a radical shift in theological emphasis during the late medieval period between the 13th and early 14th centuries. This downplayed a previous emphasis in theological thought and spiritual practice that drew more upon the 'sacramental imagination' where God might be known 'through signs and symbols' within the material and natural world, akin to Berger's 'signals of transcendence' within human experience.[7]

While the 'technocratic imagination' of concepts and mechanism superseded the older, visual 'sacramental imagination' of signs and symbols, particularly in the spiritual practice of the western church, the takeover has never been complete. Signs and symbols remain important within Eastern Orthodox Christianity and, in part, Roman Catholic practice, along with other faith expressions too, as the 'Living with the Gods' exhibit illustrates.

The value of imagery within the faith experience has not been without controversy. In the first part of the Bible, the long story of God's pilgrimage with the people of Israel, the ten commandments stipulate, 'You shall not make for yourself an image' (Exodus 20:4). There is a fear that images of the divine might become objects of worship in themselves, which continues into the New Testament. As Paul warns in the opening lines of his letter to the early Christian communities of Rome in the first century: 'The glory of the immortal God [was exchanged] for images made to look like a mortal human being and birds and animals and reptiles' (Romans 1:23).

The Christian faith arose at a time when ancient visual arts had reached a height not seen in previous cultures. As found within the collection of the British Museum, portraiture in Greek and Roman traditions was not bettered until the advent of the photographic camera 1,800 years later. Connection of such art with pagan religion led to a continued suspicion in the early church of the visualisation of faith. The rise of Islam through the 8th century, with its strong rejection of the use of images in religious practice, also stoked resistance to the use of imagery with Christian worship.

While the use of imagery in Christian worship nevertheless survived, namely in Eastern Orthodox iconography, within western Christianity greater suspicion remained. The Synod of Paris of 824 accepted that images served an ornamental purpose – akin to today's use of imagery to enhance engagement with worship – yet warned against seeing them as having power to bring about salvation.

Nevertheless, in an age of mass illiteracy, imagery continued to be valued as a teaching tool to convey the Bible narrative. The Franciscan movement, arising in the 13th century, also sought to encounter God through nature, while earlier Celtic Christianity on the western fringe of Europe used carved and painted geometrical shapes, along with images of Christ and nature, on stone crosses. Debate continued through the age of the Reformation. Martin Luther tolerated images within worship and devotion; John Calvin described them as a book for idiots.

The debate over imagery continued through to the 20th century, being crystalised in the contrasting opinions of Karl Barth and Emil Brunner over the nature of revelation and grace. For Barth, art, culture and religion were the three great powers by which humanity contradicted the grace of God. Any revelation arising from within the human or natural world detracted from God's direct revelation through scripture. While Brunner agreed that humanity's quest for the divine was futile apart from God's revelation, he viewed such cultural expressions as a sign of longing for divine encounter, so providing a point of contact for God's word to be known.

One hundred years later, this debate remains unresolved. It may ever be so, the two contrasting poles needing to be held in creative and imaginative tension. This tension arises because words and images as human constructions from within creation are both incapable of fully expressing the divine life which lies beyond, yet is entwined, with creation.

What you see is what you get

The shift from a sacramental to technocratic view of the world played a part in limiting seeing the divine through art and the natural world. Theological debate as to the nature of divine revelation also clouded the view. And a further shift in perspective in the 18th century dimmed it further.

Resisting the technocratic view, expressions of art within the Eastern Orthodox world remained primarily symbolic, as exemplified by icons. To prevent idolatry, where the divine is seen as being present within an object's form, from the early centuries of the church, icons were painted to a prescribed formula that aimed to allow divine light to shine through their beauty.[8] Their background lacked realism and dynamism, acting only to identify and frame the central human figures – Christ, Mary or a saint – and their spiritual significance and story. This creates a point within the material world through which the divine beauty shines, inviting prayer within the viewer.

In contrast, from the 13th century onwards, western painting increasingly focused on realistic expression, shaped in part by the shift from a sacramental to a technocratic approach to knowing. Orthodox thinkers viewed such realistic expression as limiting the ability of art to express the transcendent. Yet, up to and during the Renaissance, western styles of art were still viewed as being able to provide a connection with God. Michelangelo saw in the creativity of the artist an imitation of divine creativity, and the potential in art of perceiving 'beauty in God's creation that otherwise might pass [the viewer] by'.[9]

Despite stylistic differences, both eastern and western art retained the idea that beauty conveyed a sense of the divine essence. Yet, this long-held view, arising from the ancient Greeks, was challenged by the Enlightenment thinker Immanuel Kant in the 18th century. The phrase 'beauty is in the eye of the beholder' is often used to express the personal preferences of like and dislike that people have when viewing art or choosing the décor and furniture for their homes. Yet, when first coined by Kant, it conveyed a deeper meaning. He argued that what you see is what you get. The beauty someone might see in a work of art, object or in nature was not a signal of a deeper, transcendent meaning. Rather, the perception of beauty arose solely from how the physical object stirred the emotion of the viewer, leading to a judgement that it was pleasing to look at. As a conveyor of divine essence, beauty and, with it, art are sent along the road to Coventry.

God has given us a book full of 'pictures'

When I was a child, I went to Sunday school at a Baptist church. To encourage us to come regularly, we were awarded an annual prize for good attendance: a book, with an ornate sheet stuck inside the front cover marking our achievement. I still have and treasure these books.

The first was a picture book of farm animals, with coloured prints of children visiting a farm. You might say it was a celebration of God's wonderful creation. In the following years, it was often a 'Ladybird Easy Reader,' again full of wonderfully detailed coloured prints accompanying a simple page of writing – first, *The Birth of Jesus*, followed the next year by *A First Book of Saints*. With stories of real saints, like St Andrew, and more mythical ones, like St George, you might think it was a strange book for a Baptist Sunday school prize; Baptists don't really celebrate the saints! Then, I moved on to history books – *James I and the Gunpowder Plot*. I'm not sure what this says about ecumenical relationships in the 1960s in the town I grew up in, but in its defence, the story of the King James Bible was recounted in its final pages.

I remember, too, a hymn we used to sing in those days. You don't hear it so often now, although it appears from time to time as people reminisce in 'Songs of Praise' services. It begins: 'God has given us a book full of stories', inspiring delight in the Bible. For while the Bible is not a picture book, it is a book full of pictures.

In common with other monotheistic faiths originating within the Middle East, in Christianity a written text, shaped by human creativity and culture, is seen as a divinely inspired bearer of revelation. However, this written revelation flows from the central act of God's revelation – the incarnation. God is encountered not only through written word but in the divine being expressed within creation: 'The Word became flesh and made his dwelling among us' (John 1:14). We encounter the divine not only through hearing or reading Jesus' story, but through all the senses. As the writer of the first letter of John says: 'We declare to you what was from the beginning, what we have heard, what we have seen with our eyes, what we have looked at and touched with our hands, concerning the word of life' (1 John 1:1–2, NRSV). Hearing, touch and sight.

Within the Eastern Orthodox Church, the incarnation provides a basis for an emphasis upon a visual encounter with God. Yet even before the moment of the incarnation, the Bible story recounts numerous occurrences where God is encountered in visual ways, such as the rainbow at the conclusion of the flood story in Genesis, a sign of God's continuing care for the whole Earth (Genesis 9:15). And Job, mentioned back in chapter 1, who meets God through the wonder, diversity and mystery of creation, responds: 'My ears had heard of you but now my eyes have seen you' (Job 42:5).

In the gospels, Jesus' own teaching technique is also very visual. Rather than concepts, his parables draw on the visual, painting imaginative, vivid word pictures that rely on the prior visual experiences of their hearers. Through them, Jesus imaginatively connects everyday events and objects with the character and action of God. When asked about the purpose of parables, Jesus replies: 'The reason I speak to them in parables is that "seeing they do not perceive, and hearing they do not listen, nor do they understand"' (Matthew 13:13, NRSV). Commenting upon this, Cheryl Forbes suggests that through the parables, Jesus seeks to 'expand the imaginations of his followers', enabling them to see in a new way, beyond rational modes of understanding. C.H. Dodd also sees discovery as the central purpose of parables, their metaphors 'drawn from nature or common life… leaving the mind in sufficient doubt about its precise application to tease it into active thought'.[10]

Today, with the internet, social media, videography and smart phones, there has been a resurgence of the use of art and photography of the natural world in worship and spiritual practice across a wide range of Christian traditions, stimulating prayer, illustrating Bible readings and song lyrics. Yet, unlike art in the past, it mostly remains in the background, a support act to verbal communication. There is little attempt to engage with the image as an experience through which God may be encountered. We might describe it like a Christian Instagram, where images form a backdrop on which to share life experiences.

While shifts in the way the world is viewed and known may have clouded the idea of seeing God within art and the natural world, Jesus' imaginative use of images from everyday life and nature in his parables holds the hope of a sunnier view. And stretching our imagination into the present day, the placing of the statue of Nataraja within the grounds of CERN hints that an imaginative, visual exploration of the relationship between science and faith may prove fruitful.

Perhaps, through the images that science provides, something of God's nature, purpose and activity might still be perceived through an imaginative engagement which renews our thinking and seeing. This would foster a reawakened appreciation of God's gift of science, expanding our vision of God's precious natural world. And it might even stimulate the imagination of those who have sent God to Coventry, so that within the wonder of the natural world, they might see something of the divine.

3

Art, science and God

Planet watching – art or science?

London is full of excellent museums encompassing many fields of human knowledge. In the same year that I took my first trip to Coventry, together with others in my school year group, I went on a cultural trip down to London. We were given a choice: a visit to The National Gallery on Trafalgar Square or to the Science Museum and the Natural History Museum.

With my growing passion for science, it was a no-brainer and off to the Science Museum in South Kensington I went. Little did I know that a few years later I would be living in London, studying at Imperial College just around the corner. Both the Science Museum and the Natural History Museum next door were places I took time out from my studies to visit through those years. They are cathedrals that reflect the success of 'technocratic imagination', visually displaying human scientific and technological achievements across different fields, from exploring the vastness of the universe to glimpsing its smallest scales. They display human ingenuity and imagination, enabling amazing machines to be built and the natural processes of life to be understood.

Many years later, I found myself back at the Natural History Museum with a friend from those school days. We had long shared an interest in space, and that afternoon we visited a new exhibit, 'Other Worlds', exploring the planets of our solar system. Observed as 'wandering stars' since ancient times, in the 15th century Galileo gave us a new perspective on planets as he turned his small telescope to the night sky, seeing them as discs rather than points of light as stars appear. Yet, despite larger and larger telescopes being built through the following centuries, even in the mid-20th century, photographs of planets revealed few details of their surface features.

In my teens, looking up at Jupiter through my own small telescope from my parent's back garden, my view was little different from that of Galileo centuries before. I could see its four large 'Galilean' moons – Europa, Ganymede, Callisto and Io – dancing around the central disc of the huge gas giant across several weeks of observation. I could see maybe a few of the cloud bands that encircle its globe; yet even its famous Great Red Spot, a storm that has persisted for centuries, was hard to see.

From my school years to the present day, robotic space probes have transformed our vision of the planets that orbit the Sun along with the Earth, beyond even the imagination of earlier astronomers. No longer are they dim

3

Art, science and God

Planet watching – art or science?

London is full of excellent museums encompassing many fields of human knowledge. In the same year that I took my first trip to Coventry, together with others in my school year group, I went on a cultural trip down to London. We were given a choice: a visit to The National Gallery on Trafalgar Square or to the Science Museum and the Natural History Museum.

With my growing passion for science, it was a no-brainer and off to the Science Museum in South Kensington I went. Little did I know that a few years later I would be living in London, studying at Imperial College just around the corner. Both the Science Museum and the Natural History Museum next door were places I took time out from my studies to visit through those years. They are cathedrals that reflect the success of 'technocratic imagination', visually displaying human scientific and technological achievements across different fields, from exploring the vastness of the universe to glimpsing its smallest scales. They display human ingenuity and imagination, enabling amazing machines to be built and the natural processes of life to be understood.

Many years later, I found myself back at the Natural History Museum with a friend from those school days. We had long shared an interest in space, and that afternoon we visited a new exhibit, 'Other Worlds', exploring the planets of our solar system. Observed as 'wandering stars' since ancient times, in the 15th century Galileo gave us a new perspective on planets as he turned his small telescope to the night sky, seeing them as discs rather than points of light as stars appear. Yet, despite larger and larger telescopes being built through the following centuries, even in the mid-20th century, photographs of planets revealed few details of their surface features.

In my teens, looking up at Jupiter through my own small telescope from my parent's back garden, my view was little different from that of Galileo centuries before. I could see its four large 'Galilean' moons – Europa, Ganymede, Callisto and Io – dancing around the central disc of the huge gas giant across several weeks of observation. I could see maybe a few of the cloud bands that encircle its globe; yet even its famous Great Red Spot, a storm that has persisted for centuries, was hard to see.

From my school years to the present day, robotic space probes have transformed our vision of the planets that orbit the Sun along with the Earth, beyond even the imagination of earlier astronomers. No longer are they dim can science be art in the way that human artistic works have been a vehicle of divine revelation through the centuries? If so, how should such 'art' be seen for the transcendent to be encountered beyond the more fixed, objective meaning that science points to? While scientific images are 'signs', pointing to an ordered, rational description of the natural world, might they have the potential to become 'symbols', pointing beyond the material to the divine artist behind creation?

The East says no. Well, maybe.

From the perspective of some Eastern Orthodox commentators, when it comes to science being art, the answer is no! In *The Art of the Icon*, Orthodox theologian Paul Evdokimov contrasts icons with scientific imagery. He judges that icons are never meant to be a window upon nature as scientific images are. In an icon, the background of the image provides only the stage on which the central human figure is brought to the fore, representing a well-known person or story of faith. Together, image and story evoke prayer and divine encounter within the viewer. In this way, they are an example of the 'sacramental' imagination.

Conversely, scientific images as windows upon nature reveal the material world in detail beyond the ability of human senses to perceive without the aid of technology. Wondrous they may be, resonating with the ancient song that speaks of the heavens declaring the glory of God (Psalm 19:1), yet they represent a perception of nature in which its 'mystic heart has been cut out…

[being] completely beyond science's capacity to grasp'.[13] They are a product of the technological imagination.

However, in contrast, reflecting on the Orthodox practice of praying with icons, Jim Forest notes the shared ability of icons and images of creation to evoke a sense of awe. This is an experience that is common to people of faith and none, which he suggests is akin to prayer and a moment when the divine is encountered.[14] So, can science's window on nature be art? Well, maybe.

The West says maybe too. But then again…

Western Christianity also asks the same question of science. Zachary Hayes ponders: 'Is it possible… to look out at the physical cosmos with the lens of contemporary science… [and see] the manifest mystery of God?'[15] In asking such a question, Hayes reflects his Franciscan tradition, which since its origins in the 13th century has been shaped by a sacramental imaginative vision of the world.

Francis and his followers popularised a much earlier nature mysticism originating in the fifth- and sixth-century writings of the anonymous Greek Christian Denys the Areopagite. Denys' spirituality was 'deeply sensitive to the manifold variety of God's… inexhaustible being in creation'.[16] It resonated with Paul's words to the city elders during his visit to Athens: 'God who made the world and everything in it is the Lord of heaven and earth and… in him we live and move and have our being' (Acts 17:24, 28). It is a spirituality that is an expression of panentheism, as distinct from pantheism. While the latter sees all material objects and beings as divine, panentheism holds that while God and the material creation are distinct, creation is held and shaped within the life and love of God.

Later in the New Testament, writings attributed to Paul hint at this divine embrace of creation. The letter to the Colossians, speaking of the creation of the world, says of Jesus the Son: 'All things have been created through him and for him. He is before all things, and in him all things hold together' (Colossians 1:16–17). Despite its fallenness, creation is still able to express a likeness of divine being, a facet which finds its fullest expression in the incarnation: 'In the beginning was the Word, and the Word was with God, and the Word was God… The Word became flesh and made his dwelling among us. We have seen his glory, the glory of the one and only Son, who came from the Father, full of grace and truth' (John 1:1, 14).

Hayes, in searching for an answer to his question as to whether God might be glimpsed within science's vision of the cosmos, draws upon the thoughts of a successor to Francis as leader of the Franciscan movement, the theologian Bonaventure. He was born in 1221 in the precarious hilltop town of Civita de Bagnoregio, now in the Italian province of Lazio, to the north of Rome. A UNESCO World Heritage site, the beautiful village lies on top of an eroding column of volcanic rock. Entrance is via a modern bridge, easing the need for tourists to clamber up a steep, crumbling cliff. His family home has long since dropped off the side of the hill. An iron staircase leads you to what was the cellar, although to be honest, on my visit, I didn't fancy a trek down the flimsy iron runs. Visiting such a wonderful place, one can understand how the wonder of the vista looking out and over the surrounding countryside might provoke a sense of divine presence.

Bonaventure's most well-known work is *The Soul's Journey to God*, in which he sets out a programme as to how people might grow towards expressing the likeness of Christ. On this pilgrimage, the first step is the contemplation of 'vestiges' – windows within creation that enable signs of the divine presence to be seen. In his vision, such windows have three panes – a triptych – linked to the Christian trinitarian view of God as Father, Son and Holy Spirit. Firstly, the existence of creation is a symbol of God's creative power. Secondly, divine wisdom is displayed by the sheer diversity of the material forms of creation and its creatures, each reflecting in part an echo of the fullness of the Incarnation. Finally, the perceived purpose of an object or creature and its relationship with other elements of creation hints of God's ultimate purpose for creation, to be united fully within the love of God.

For Bonaventure, that the character and being of God might be glimpsed through the material world was a no-brainer: 'Who[ever] does not allow [them]self to be illuminated by the glory of created things is blind.'[17] For him, 'the entire cosmos… [was] a vast symbol of [divine being]… a work of art that expresses the divine idea in something that is not God'.[18] Despite the limited way people of Bonaventure's day could explore the material world through unaided human senses alone, his view opens a way for the images of science to be art in the sense that they provide a window upon the divine, but perhaps not in the way Bonaventure was so confident in.

When one window closes, another opens

Through the early centuries of the church, theological exploration of the Bible was assisted by thinkers from the ancient Greek world, primarily Aristotle and Plato. This heritage was helpful in providing tools to explore the experience and meaning of the mystery of the incarnation in Jesus. These Greek thinkers enabled the church, living within a Roman culture that drew much on their ideas, to provide an effective apologetic to defend the new faith in the face of the dominant and older religious movements.

Part of this Greek heritage was an appreciation of beauty in culture and nature. Inspired by the thinking of Plato, Bonaventure, and many of his contemporaries, saw beauty as a reflection of the greater, perfect beauty of God. Within the modern scientific world, an echo of this view still holds sway. Scientific exploration and writing often employs classical notions of beauty, such as symmetry, elegance and harmony, among others, as indications of whether an idea or theory is to be preferred over another. So, looking for Bonaventure's vestiges within the beauty of science's imagery might enable it to be art in the sense of evoking divine encounter.

Well, let's not be too hasty! Ede observes that 'contemporary scientists often talk about "beauty" [whereas] artists hardly ever do'.[19] The scientific vision of the cosmos has developed remarkedly since the Enlightenment of the 17th century, when Newton laid down his laws of motion and gravity that provided a unified explanation of the motion of objects both in everyday experience and across the night sky. These ideas have now been supplemented by Einstein's theory of gravity, exploring the largest scales of the cosmos, along with quantum theory's weird take on the smallest. Yet, the continual appeal to notions of beauty suggests a lack of insight within the scientific community as to how the ability of art to convey meaning and truth has developed through the centuries alongside it. For remember, as Immanuel Kant remarked, 'beauty is in the eye of the beholder'.

Kant sent beauty as a mark of divine presence to Coventry, and Bonaventure's notion of vestiges with it. In place of beauty, Kant emphasised the experience of the sublime. He focused on the sense that when one looks at an object or vista, there is more to see than what is immediately presented, more than can be rationally comprehended. This is an experience common to people of faith and none, often described as awe and wonder. It might arise from looking upon a majestic mountain range or watching the setting sun sink below the horizon. Or looking up, trying to catch fleeting meteors in their final fiery journey across the sky after eons travelling through the coldness of space. Similarly, and perhaps evoking a deeper sense of awe, observing the shimmering curtain of the green-and-pink aurora painting the northern horizon, as subatomic particles sent out by the Sun and guided by the Earth's magnetic field crash into the atmosphere, causing it to glow.

And yet, there is nothing deeper to see here. With Kant, what you saw is what you got. As with beauty, feelings associated with the sublime arise solely within a person rather than as a response to an external divine presence. Nevertheless, as Jesus' parables hold out hope for divine encounter via the imagination, as an imaginative construction, Bonaventure's concept of vestiges within creation might still have value in facilitating divine encounter.

The visual encounter of the finite world that gives rise to an experience of awe and wonder marks a moment when the human mind fails to interpret the experience within a rational framework. It is an experience that either remains a mystery to the viewer or one that is commonly explained in terms of divine encounter. Even if the experience or encounter is within a person, evoked by seeing nature rather than seeing through it to something deeper, it may still provide space and a point of contact for God to be revealed through the windows of Bonaventure's vestiges. The vision of science might be art after all – even an icon through which God is encountered.

Exercising the imagination

When I was a child

Lego! Along with many children through the past 50 years or so, I love it! I remember having an old biscuit tin full of the multicoloured bricks. I still feel sad when I think back about how that tin was passed on to younger members of my family after I left home. I've no idea where it ended up. It is still a delight to visit the Lego store in London's Leicester Square, to look at the large models constructed out of thousands of little plastic bricks, along with the massive range of kits available these days. From the natural beauty of flowers to iconic buildings from around the globe; from cars, aeroplanes, characters and scenes from the latest blockbuster movies to complex engineering constructions with working engines. And then there are the rockets!

In recent years, I have built a small collection of Lego rockets. I have built the towering Saturn V of the Moon landing programme of the 1960–70s, along with the fragile, spindly Lunar Module that carried Neil Armstrong and Buzz Aldrin down to the Moon's surface on 20 July 1969. These objects take me back to events that captured my imagination and led me towards a life in science.

Mind you, Lego was much simpler then: mainly coloured square and rectangular bricks, with simple windows, doors and roof tiles to enable houses to be built, plus a few wheels for cars and trucks. While simpler, it encouraged play in a different way to the exciting, detailed kits of today. Many of today's kits may foster imaginative storytelling, bounded by the stories of books and films they derive from, yet the simpler forms stimulated exploration of the creative imagination beyond this to design and construction.

Imagination is often thought to be the stuff of childhood, left behind once adulthood comes. As Paul said in his letter to the early Christians in the city of Corinth: 'When I was a child, I talked like a child, I thought like a child, I reasoned like a child. When I became [an adult], I put the ways of childhood behind me' (1 Corinthians 13:11). Now, you could accuse me of using this text imaginatively. Of course, Paul was using the transition between childhood and adulthood as a metaphor to contrast our partial understanding of God now in this life and the fuller understanding beyond death, rather than a comment on the inadequacy of the imagination. Yet, the use of metaphors, when an idea or object is described in terms of something more familiar to the listener, reader or viewer, is an imaginative act. Their common use suggests that imagination is not something one leaves behind in childhood but something that continues to play an important part in how we understand the world throughout life.

Faithful imagination?

Imagination plays a huge role in our lives. The popularity of novels – fictional stories drawing upon everyday experiences or playing with the concept of reality, as in old folk tales or science fiction – speaks of the imagination in both the writer and reader. Music, too, imaginatively conveys emotion, feelings or the experience of time and place. Still, suspicion of the imagination remains. It is often associated with illusion and falsehood, even delusion. The rational attack on belief in God through the past three centuries, seeing it as wishful thinking, an imaginative human construct or illusion, has perhaps added to distrust of imagination in the realm of faith.

The debate in the last century between Karl Barth and Emil Brunner can be seen as one over the role of imagination in encountering God. Downplaying human creative activities in the fields of art, music and theatre, Barth's stress upon the importance of the written text of the Bible is a resistance to the role imagination can play in divine revelation. The theologian Garrett Green, in considering the role imagination might play in the life of faith, follows Barth's view. While recognising that imagination plays a part in the development of the Bible, and acknowledging it is filled with imaginative word pictures to explore God's nature and actions, he believes the work of theology is to move from metaphor to universal concepts: 'Metaphors are potential concepts; concepts are petrified metaphors.'[20]

And yet, Green admits, people don't live in fully conceptual worlds. The teaching of concepts needs to be complemented by the creation of new metaphors that enhance understanding and communication. One of the challenges every preacher knows is the pressure to conjure up relevant and attention-grabbing sermon illustrations. Often drawn from life or popular culture, they attempt to recast conceptual ideas into images that enable people to grasp the meaning of the biblical text or story. Within my own Baptist tradition, it is often the 'children's talk', using an activity or a story to explore an aspect of faith, that people recall weeks, even years later, while the sermon is long forgotten!

While recognising there is a falsehood in imagination, Kant chose not to send it to Coventry along with beauty. He believed imagination played a significant role in memory, for example, in recalling an object previously encountered but not presently there and enabling anticipation of the future based upon previous experience. Before you walk through a closed door into the lounge of a house, your imagination allows you to anticipate what you might find there – easy chairs, a coffee table, TV. You may even imagine what the décor might be. You may also be surprised, for things may not be exactly as you imagined them. And, of course, in expressing your like or surprise, you need to bear in mind what Kant said: 'Beauty is in the eye of the beholder.'

Timothy Radcliffe suggests that recently the word 'imagination' has come 'to mean just the way that someone sees the world… the prism through which we view reality'.[21] In building this view, imagination plays a crucial role in compiling in the mind the experiences of difference senses, over space and time, to build a synthetic picture of reality. While this again hints at falsehood, in that it is not necessarily a full depiction of experience or material reality, it may allow the world to be seen in new ways which remain hidden when a purely material and rational view of the world is taken.

Beyond the value of imagination within the human experience of the world, resonating with Brunner's view, Roman Catholic approaches to theology and spirituality more than Protestant ones have embraced the role of the imagination in encountering God through experience of life, creation and culture, complementing written revelation. Viewing an object, either religious or secular, watching a play, reading a book, or experiencing the natural world can bring an awareness of something beyond the material experience of the moment or place. The 20th-century theologian Karl Rahner, reflecting upon the long history of Roman Catholic tradition, suggests that when an object or event is encountered through the senses, physical reality is exceeded by the imagination. Looking beyond the material experience leads to a sense of 'wonderment', opening a door to encounter with the divine presence.[22] This is only possible because human beings are made in the image of God.

Imagination – where the divine and human meet

In the Bible's creation story, the interior working of God's mind is revealed. God says, 'Let us make mankind in our image, in our likeness' (Genesis 1:26). This statement of intent reveals that the act of creation is no accident but is the result of divine forethought. From a rational perspective, it speaks of God's design of creation. Indeed, the idea that humans are shaped in terms of the image of God has often been viewed in terms of the ability to reason. Yet, such intent and design can also be cast as a creative act of the divine imagination: material creation originates as ideas imagined within the mind of God.

Through most of Christian history, the capacity to enter a relationship with God and share in the divine life has been seen as the predominant way of understanding the meaning of humanity being made in the image of God – the Imago Dei. Yet, the work of imagination in our minds plays a significant role in how we perceive ourselves, how we see others and how we see the world around us. It shapes our hopes and dreams for the future and our sorrow and remorse over the past – the 'what ifs'. It is in these imaginings that God so often meets us, bringing reassurance, comfort and hope. Cheryl Forbes describes humanity as 'imagination incarnated'. The world of the imagination is a key point of contact with the divine, the 'Imago Dei in us… [allowing] us to know God, receive his grace, worship him and see life through his eyes'.[23]

As we saw in a previous chapter, in the pages of the Bible, God is revealed to humanity through imaginative language. The Psalms are crammed with imaginative metaphors. God's protection is described as a bird protecting her young: 'He will cover you with his feathers, and under his wings you will find refuge' (Psalm 91:4). Jesus draws upon this image as he glimpses Jerusalem at the start of Holy Week: 'Jerusalem, Jerusalem… how often I have longed to gather your children together, as a hen gathers her chicks under her wings' (Matthew 23:37). And during the last supper, everyday bread and wine become symbols of Jesus' sacrifice, a sacrament of divine encounter through the material world.

It's like...

So, how does the imaginative world of metaphors work? How do they communicate meaning? The power of such use of language has been known from the time of the ancient Greeks. Aristotle defined metaphors as giving something a name that belongs to something else. For example, an athlete might be said to 'run like the wind', or it might be said of someone's difficulty in managing their finances that 'money slips through their fingers like water'. Such descriptions conjure up images in the mind, conveying one person's view and understanding to another.

Yet metaphors go beyond the use of words as descriptors or simply conveyors of information. They also involve personal engagement, of both the one from whom the idea originates and those who receive it. As the old saying goes, 'it takes two to tango'. For both, forming and receiving the metaphor draws upon their previous experience and memories. Connecting the two parts of the saying together leads to new possibilities and understanding through an act of the imagination. Such personal involvement in drawing meaning from metaphors means that they resist being reduced to a set of literal conceptual statements. This fluidity is part of the power of metaphor – but it raises difficulties too.[24]

With dependence upon imagination, the received meaning of a metaphor may be different from that intended by the originator. In the example of 'they run like the wind', while the person speaking the phrase may mean to conjure up an image of a person running fast, the one hearing it may think of a gentle breeze, leading to a different impression. If the hearer is shaped by a different cultural context than that of the speaker, either in space or time, this can result in a shift of meaning or for meaning not to be perceived at all.

For example, in the letter of James in the Bible, the image of a small rudder steering a large boat is used to describe the power of words (James 3:4). Yet, if the reader has never come across such a boat, it will be hard for them to draw meaning from the comparison. It may be necessary to recast the original metaphor into an equivalent idea that is familiar to the hearer or reader. However, this assumes that the intended meaning of the original metaphor is understood, which is not always guaranteed as it relies both on the context from which the phrase originated and on an understanding of the imaginative working of the person who created it. Nevertheless, despite such difficulties, Jesus' use of metaphors in the parables suggests their value. Jesus stretched the imagination of his hearers so that they might encounter God; the imaginative re-casting of metaphors today may allow a similar encounter with the imaginative God.

Artistic and scientific imagination

While metaphors are often expressed through words, they are commonly expressed in visual language – so called word-pictures – that draw upon the experience and memory of the person listening. Beyond words, visual art too can function as a metaphor. In creating a painting, an artist does more than convey the details of the scene before them. As well as the material nature of the person, object or scene, they bring to the process of creation their emotions and experience of the moment, together with their perceived meaning of what they see and experience of that place and moment. This is all imaginatively shaped using colour and light, the framing of the image, what is brought to the fore, what is left out. The resulting image transmits this imaginative process to others, whose own context, emotions and experiences shape the way they receive the image and perceive meaning from it, which may be similar or different from that intended by the artist.[25]

The continued use of visual art through the history of Christian spirituality suggests that amid this complex interaction lies the possibility of the divine presence being mediated through the imagination. While the process of creating and viewing art imaginatively draws upon the depths of human experience, if it is to provide a focus for divine encounter, then at the heart of the relationship between the one sharing and the one receiving must lie God, known or unknown: a meeting of the imaginative Imago Dei with the divine imagination.[26]

Yet we need to return to the question of whether the imagery of science can be art? Can it also be a place where human and divine imagination meet? Our previous exploration of whether science imagery might function in a manner akin to art in spiritual exploration left us with a 'maybe'. While imagination is commonly associated with the production of art, it is seen as less important, even irrelevant, in the field of science. If imagination, both divine and human, is vital for divine encounter and revelation, perhaps imagination-free science cannot be art.

A common view through the first half of the 20th century was that science had sent imagination to Coventry along with God. The role of imagination was rejected. Scientific exploration was a 'work of pure detachment and objectivity, orientated only by the facts' established through a cycle of hypothesis, observation of the material world, together with the formulation of theories that explain the observations and make predictions which can be further tested. The only valid meanings were those that lay within the material realm alone.[27]

However, in the latter half of the 20th century this view of science has been challenged. Michael Polanyi and Harry Prosch suggest that imagination plays a crucial role in the practice of science. Starting from an intuitive idea, which the imagination then shapes, it proceeds forwards seeking out the best path of experimentation and observation, concluding in the form of a theory. Utilising both intuition and imagination, 'science integrates fragmentary clues to an initially unknown coherent meaning'.[28] Thomas Kuhn designates such coherent meanings 'paradigms', often resulting not from a slow accumulation of facts but through a leap of the imagination.[29]

Within science such imaginative patterns are often expressed as models, drawing upon human experience of the everyday world. However, science has increasingly opened insights into reality beyond unaided human senses, down to the small-scale quantum nature of reality and out to the vast, immense universe. In seeking a coherent understanding across these scales, new and often unpicturable ideas are employed. For example, the large-scale structure of the universe shaped by gravity is described by Einstein's General Theory of Relativity using four-dimensional space-time rather than the human experience of a three-dimensional world. Meanwhile, at the smallest scales, the defined positions of the particles of the Newtonian world are replaced by uncertainty in space and time, leading to fundamental particles of the material world being described in terms of diffuse probability functions and their behaviour in terms of both billiard ball-like particles and waves. These models extend human imagination beyond an experience of the world gained by natural, technologically unaided human senses.

However, imagination works in different ways in the arts and sciences. While models in the sciences might be compared to metaphors, as noted previously, the latter have 'personal and valuational overtones' that models do not. Furthermore, art as metaphor contains much of the creative imaginative meaning of the artist, provoking the viewer to be moved through their own imaginative response. While individual personality and style may shape the creative way science is pursued and imagination leads to the integration of scattered pieces of evidence, the 'fusion of these previously unconnected clues will thereafter be quietly accepted as a fact'[30] rather than being open to further imaginative interpretation.

Using the analogy of water, in art meaning is fluid, like the water cascading down a mountain waterfall. Its molecules are loosely connected, flowing and free. Its fall is shaped initially by the rocks over which it tumbles. As the landscape opens, it has the freedom to meander across land. Conversely, in science, meaning might be said to be like ice. The molecules of water are fixed within a lattice framework, with only limited movement. It is like a glacier, shaped by the valley yet slowly shaping all that stands before it.

If spiritual meaning is to be found through the images of science, then an unfreezing of the image is needed to allow the fluidity of the imagination to explore meaning beyond the processes and ordering of the material world that science explores. To catch a glimpse of the imagination of the divine artist expressed through creation, we need a new pair of glasses that will help us to look in a fresh way. Borrowing from Jesus' words, you might say that in seeing we might perceive and in having our imagination stretched we might understand.

5

The stuff of science and God: wonder, playfulness and order

Life through a lens

Seeing the world through a lens has played a large part in my life. At the start of my teenage years, not being able to see the blackboard at the front of the class, it was clear that I needed spectacles. Subsequently, I always know when to visit the optician for a new pair of glasses. The details of distant objects become fuzzier over time. It's not something you notice day by day, and they are still much clearer than without my glasses. Yet, it's a realisation that slowly dawns. And when I put a new pair of glasses on, with lenses adjusted to provide a clearer view, it's always a 'wow' moment. The first thing I notice is that the small twigs of trees are clearer. And if I have light-reactive lenses that dim the brightness of the sky, the details of the edges of clouds become sharper.

Others lens too have played a part in deepening my appreciation of the world. My first small telescope at eleven years of age opened a view of the night sky previously inaccessible by my naked eyes alone. Being able to see the craters and mountains of the Moon or the diffuse light of the nebula in Orion's belt and the young stars within it has never lost its wonder.

And there were glimpses of the small world, too, through the eyepiece of a microscope, watching the spinning dance of microscopic animals in pond water or the cell structure of an onion skin. These days, with the wonders of technology, I just pop a microscope adaptor on my mobile phone to look at minibeasts and details of plants around the garden.

In many ways, we take lenses for granted these days. But they open a new way of seeing, whether in the everyday or in scientific exploration. So far we've considered different ways of seeing beyond the way in which our eyes respond to physical light. We have looked at how seeing the natural world and gazing at art has played a part in spiritual exploration within the Christian faith. An important part of this is understanding the metaphoric meaning of art, and the important part that imagination plays in communicating meaning. From this, we have explored whether the frozen images of science might be made fluid to enable the divine artist of creation to be known, akin to my experience of gazing at the images in Michael Benson's 'Other Worlds' exhibit at the Natural History Museum or in the awe and wonder felt as people watch the stunning imagery of science and nature documentaries. To do this, drawing these strands together, we need a trip to the opticians for a new lens prescription.

A new lens

While lenses are everyday things, constructing the right lens for a task is a complex process. The ability of lenses to bend light depends upon their shape and the properties of the material they are made from. Convex lenses are thinner at the edge than in the centre, bringing light to a focus. Conversely, concave lenses are thinner in the middle than at their rim, dispersing light that enters it. Some materials are more optically dense, bending light through larger angles, allowing powerful lenses to be made thinner. All these factors combine to shape light in just the right way to bring things into focus.

Both Eastern Orthodox icons and Bonaventure's vestiges might be said to be visual theological lenses through which the divine might be glimpsed through material objects. Peter Berger's signals of transcendence, signs within ordinary human experience that speak of divine presence shaping the world, are another example. In constructing a lens to gaze in a fresh way at science's images of creation, as with a physical lens, we need to imaginatively bring different components together.

We will combine three of Berger's signals of transcendence – wonder, play and seeking order – with Bonaventure's three-fold vestiges – power, created diversity and purpose – which he saw as signs within the created world hinting of God's presence. Finally, we draw insights from the Eastern Orthodox use of icons – the importance of story and the capacity of the material world to convey the divine light, much as a transparent lens conveys physical light.

Wonder, playfulness and the seeking of order are common experiences across many aspects of life, yet they connect with science's specific exploration of the world. Wonder is a human response evoked by what science reveals of the cosmos. It is often the reason people decide to work within the sciences and continues to play a part in their wanting to go deeper in understanding the nature of creation. Playfulness and seeking order are also characteristics of the process of science. Creatively, scientists play with ideas and create experiments and machines to explore the cosmos. They seek to reveal the order within the universe, expressed in mathematical equations or in understanding how different things are connected to one another.

While the process of science has developed significantly over the last 300 years since the European Enlightenment, you can glimpse aspects of its development further back in history – through the Arabic mathematicians, chemists and physicists of the medieval period, drawing upon ancient Greek philosophers. You can even glimpse it in the first pages of the Bible, and the story of the first human 'Adam'. There, God 'brought [the animals] to [Adam] to see what he would name them; and whatever [Adam] called each living creature, that was its name. So [Adam] gave names to all the livestock, the birds in the sky and all the wild animals' (Genesis 2:19–20). This is a scene in which Adam creatively brings human order to the world, akin to how science does so today.

Creating wonder, being playful and bringing order: science itself could be said to be a 'signal of transcendence'. It is not something that sends God to

Coventry but a human activity that meets God's imaginative creativity. Certainly, beyond the characteristics of the human activity of science, playfulness and order seem to be inherent to the fabric of the material universe itself. In speaking of these experiences as 'signals of transcendence', Berger assumes they are implicitly connected to the possibility of encountering the supernatural divine being behind the material world. As to the nature of this being, the vision they provide is diffuse and broad. They allow light to be seen, yet like a concave lens, the resulting image is blurred.

Within a Christian perspective, this blurred image is brought to focus by combining Berger's concave lens with the convex lens of Bonaventure's idea of vestiges within creation that display the character and activity of God: God's creative power in the existence of the world; divine wisdom found within the diversity of creatures and forms in creation; and an understanding of the purpose of each creature, form or process, and its connection with the whole created order, as a sign of God's purpose in creation, drawing all things towards the love of God. This imaginative lens brings things into focus:

> God's creative **power** is connected to the experience of **wonder**.
>
> Divine wisdom, seen in the **diversity** of creation, is brought alongside **playfulness**.
>
> God's **purpose** within creation is combined with seeking **order**.

Wonder and power

Turning again to the creation story in Genesis, at the very end God 'blessed the seventh day and made it holy, because on it he rested from all the work of creating that he had done' (Genesis 2:3). Perhaps this is a moment when God stepped back and just revelled in the wonder of it all. And in the wonder of the cosmos that science reveals, whether known or unknown, we share in a holy moment with the divine being who is the source and sustainer of it all.

In her book *Wonder and Wisdom*, Celia Deane-Drummond notices this connection, suggesting wonder 'is a natural reaction to the exuberant and astonishing power of things to be, to exist at all'.[31] In this she captures a question at the heart of both science and spiritual exploration: why is there something rather than nothing? This is a disquieting question for both those of faith and those of none. One biologist who has sent God to Coventry, Richard Dawkins, acknowledges that wonder can leave a person discontented. It is a recognition that here is something beyond what is known, leading back to the response important for both science and faith: 'We don't know.' Dawkins limits this unknowing to the purely material realm, strongly denying a link to a sense of the transcendent yet recognising something positive in the experience: that it can be a powerful driver in provoking scientific exploration. From the perspective of the rational exploration of science, he suggests that the only response to 'We don't know' is 'But we are working on it.'[32]

Voices through the ages have noted contrasting responses to the experience of wonder. Teresa of Cartegena, the late-medieval Castilian mystic and Roman Catholic nun, in her book *Wonder at the Works of God,* wrote of two responses to wonder. One focused upon the phenomenon that evokes wonder, akin to Dawkin's response. The other mixed devotion and faith.[33] Similarly, three centuries later, in the 18th century, the German polymath Johann Wolfgang von Goethe valued awe and wonder as the highest of human experiences and recognised this dual perspective. While he thought people ought to 'be content to feel awe in the face of the phenomena of the natural world', he also recognised for some this was inadequate: '[They] insist on going further like children who peep in a mirror and then turn it around to see what is on the other side.'[34]

Attuned to Bonaventure's view that creation holds signs of God's presence, Deane-Drummond sees the experience of wonder inspired by creation as able to lead people 'to a sense of the transcendent… religious awe, comparable to that portrayed through religious art'.[35] This sense of being drawn beyond material description and process is, for theologian John Macquarrie, a response to the universally present God. While God is separate from creation, the divine presence imbues 'a sacramental potentiality in virtually everything'[36] in material creation. The immense power and vastness of creation points beyond mechanism and physical energy towards the divine power at work in bringing creation into being.

Yet, wonder does not respond to a past event alone, projected forward by material processes, from a moment when, as the classical Christian doctrine of *creatio ex nihilo* emphasises, something arose from nothing. This view of divine action aimed to protect the absolute difference between God and the created material world in the face of alternative views that saw God as part of the created order. Wonder is a present encounter with the divine creator's action, what Wolfhart Pannenberg describes as the continual 'eternal [creative] act of God [that] cannot be restricted to the creation of the world'[37] – *creatio continua* – stressing God's immanence and continual participation within creation. Orthodox views resonate with this view of wonder as a present encounter with God's creative activity. Bishop Seraphim Sigrist, in the book *Theology of Wonder*, recounts Rabbi Dovid Din suggesting that 'with God the act of creating and the act of sustaining are… a single action… every day is the first day of creation because creation is a gift continually arriving and opening out'.[38]

A part of wonder is a disquieting sense of unknowing that undermines our sense of significance. We are Homo sapiens: literally 'wise people'. Yet, the unknowing of the vast complexity of the world we inhabit, within a vast universe that science reveals, raises the anxiety of 'we don't know', eating into our sense of being. However, seen as a response to God's continual presence and work within the world, wonder has the capacity to affirm our sense of our significance in the face of existential threats and death that also emphasise how much 'we don't know'.

The Covid-19 pandemic is one such recent moment of 'we don't know', not in the face of the beauty of the world, but of its ugliness. It was a global sharing in a darker side of unknowing, but that can nonetheless still be a part of wonder. We shared this experience as a global community to differing degrees, yet we all face myriad equally significant moments of unknowing through the pilgrimage of our lives. Lockdown limited our contact with others, those from whom we gain much significance. And during the limited times we were allowed to move outside, many people reappreciated the value of the natural world for their well-being through its changing seasons. While in response to the collective trauma we are trying to swiftly put the experience of the crisis behind us, one thing we need to hang on to and deepen is our appreciation of how the wonder of creation can affirm our significance.

Science tells the story of the mystery of the continual arising of something in the face of decay towards nothing. Yet, beyond Dawkins' response to the unknowing of wonder – 'we are working on it' – the wonder that science evokes invites encounter with the divine artist and storyteller, continually active and present in creation. This is the one who in the experience of wonder continually invites us to stand alongside them on the ever-present final holy day of the creation story, looking at all that is made and calling it 'very good'. Despite our sense of the brokenness of the world, wonder as ever-present sabbath is part of lived experience and leads us to know that we are a significant part of creation.

Playfulness and diversity

On his voyage around the world on *HMS Beagle*, expedition naturalist Charles Darwin spent time studying the flora and fauna of the Galapagos Islands, isolated volcanic outcrops on the equator in the eastern Pacific Ocean. He was amazed at the diversity of plants and animals to be found across the small chain of islands. In his journal, he struggled with the question: 'Why the creator would have made so many species in such a small area?'[39] What he saw there profoundly affected his view of the natural world, inspiring the development of his ideas on evolution in the celebrated 1859 book *On the Origin of Species*.

You don't have to travel to the other side of the world to appreciate the vast variety of life found across the Earth, both in the present and through its long pilgrimage. Preserved in ancient marble, diverse forms of life can be seen across the floor of Coventry Cathedral. And at the bottom of our garden, among the branches of a small willow tree, through the summer months I have marvelled as a carpet of grey willow aphids colonised its branches. The largest aphid in the UK, they inhabit willow species, drawing nourishment from its sap. Their presence attracts predator ladybirds, hunting for a snack, while in the sunlight, small, sugary drops of honey dew drop from the aphids, coating the lower branches and attracting small hover flies, wasps and larger European hornets. A diverse, wonderful ecosystem found within a few square metres.

Darwin's *On the Origin of Species* and the later development of evolutionary ideas have played their part in sending God to Coventry. Its publication led to the famous 1860 debate between Thomas Huxley and the then bishop of Oxford, Samuel Wilberforce, at Oxford's Museum of Natural History. Over a century later, in the nearby University Church of St Mary the Virgin, biochemist and theologian Arthur Peacocke, in his 1978 Bampton lecture 'Creation and the world of science', suggested an answer to Darwin's musings. The diversity of life found across the Earth is 'the overflow of divine generosity… [God] displaying the delight and sheer exuberance of play in the unceasing act of creation.'[40]

As my love of Lego suggests, the activity of play goes far beyond our childhood years. Nor is it a wasteful and frivolous activity. Play has learning potential, recognised in the early years school system. In play children mimic what they see of the world around them, forming patterns of behaviour and learning new skills. Play is also expressed through sport and games, which bring thousands to stadiums and see millions watching the Olympics and Paralympics. Literature, music and art play with words and ideas, sounds and light, capturing human stories, longings and emotions. Less highbrow, I recently spent an evening playing crazy golf with a group of friends, laughing together as we navigated an indoor course themed around tropical islands. It was a moment to build relationship and discover more of ourselves and one another.

Deeper still, play shapes our being and culture. Dutch cultural historian Johan Huizinga describes human beings as 'Homo ludens' – playful people, complementing our description as Homo sapiens, wise people. Play is an activity and characteristic that is not limited to our species alone. Audiences of nature documentaries delight in watching animals playing in a seemingly human way: lion cubs, tumbling and wrestling with one another; dolphins and whales jumping through the air, twisting and turning, for no apparent reason other than the joy of it. While this play might be our imposition of human characteristics upon creatures who are clearly not human, Huizinga suggests that 'animals have not waited for [humans] to teach them their playing'.[41]

Peter Berger sees the human propensity for play as providing a place of encounter with the divine presence. Huizinga and others have also noted the transcendental possibilities of play. In a study of children's spirituality, Rebecca Nye suggests that play 'can draw us into uncharted waters (imagination, deeper relationships)... [having] sacred qualities'.[42] With playful creativity being a part of many aspects of culture, such as art, it opens the possibility of divine encounter. Playful imagination is also a part of science, important in the development of hypothesis, experimental design, interpretation of data and formation of models, as well as in the relational nature of scientific discussion and argument.

This playful aspect of science's view of the material world allows 'Homo ludens' to encounter 'Deus ludens' – the playful God. In *Theology and Joy*, Jürgen Moltmann suggests play is part of the being and activity of God within creation. Creation is not a necessity but is grounded in God's good will and pleasure: 'Creation is God's play, a play of his groundless and inscrutable wisdom.'[43] The wisdom literature of the Old Testament alludes to divine playfulness in descriptions of divine wisdom in the act of creation: 'Then I was a little child at his side. I was filled with delight day after day, rejoicing always in his presence, rejoicing in his whole world and delighting in the human race' (Proverbs 8:30–31, see NIV footnote). God invites human beings to partake in this playfulness as Adam imaginatively names the animals in the biblical stories of creation. This playfulness continues to be expressed through science's ordering of diverse reality from a human perspective.

This ancient story of the interplay of humanity, God and other creatures is still a present experience. Robert Johnson sees encounter with the playful God through creation as a moment when people might 'commune joyfully with creation and our fellow creatures… becom[ing] aware that life is truly a gift from God'.[44] This resonates with Bonaventure's second vestige in creation, namely the vast range and diversity of created forms as a sign and expression of the wisdom of God. Diversity flows from God's playful imagination and wisdom within the mind of God, expressed into being through God's creative word. The ultimate expression of that word is The Word, the second person of the Trinity: 'the image of the invisible God, the firstborn over all creation,' in whom 'all things were created' (Colossians 1:15–16). Jesus, incarnated as a human being, expresses the fullness of God within creation. Likewise, all other created things originating within the imagination of God hold a likeness to divine ideas, so having sacramental potential to reveal something of the mind of the divine artist.

Projecting Bonaventure's ideas into the present, Franciscan Zachary Hayes comments that 'the entire cosmos can be seen as a vast symbol of God… a work of art that expresses the divine idea in something that is not God'. He goes on to suggest that 'if Bonaventure were to pick-up the writings of some twentieth century cosmologist', such as the esteemed Stephen Hawking, and hear them speak as science revealing 'the mind of God', Bonaventure 'would no doubt resonate with the language, though he would have a fundamental[ly] different understanding of what the language means'.[45] Rather than science's focus upon cataloguing the diversity of forms and processes of the material world, Bonaventure would see playful creation as a natural icon, a divine window facilitating transcendental encounter. Science allows the reading of such natural icons with fresh eyes, created playfulness meeting the playfulness of God. As Robert Ellis suggests: 'Deus ludens creates and enters into relationship with Homo ludens',[46] revealing further insight into the meaning of humanity as Imago Dei.

Order and purpose

Milton Keynes, the city where I live, is a very ordered place. You might say that about all human settlements compared to the wildness of the natural world, but Milton Keynes is more ordered than most in England. It's a new city, just over 50 years old, designed around a regular grid of roads running north–south and east–west, connected at their many junctions by roundabouts.

As well as being home to over a quarter of a million people, its roads and many buildings are set within a forest of one million trees. When we first came to Milton Keynes 20 years ago, the verges and central reservation were well trimmed and mowed. Over the years, that has changed. Globally, the diversity of natural ecosystems has reduced by over 50% through the 50-year life of the new city. Much of this decline is linked to urban expansion and the conversion of wilderness areas into farmland to support growing urban populations. In response to this, in recent years, on many of the road verges and roundabouts in Milton Keynes, the grass and wildflowers have been allowed to grow up, only being mowed at certain times of year, encouraging greater biodiversity.

Milton Keynes is a little like Marmite. Some people love it. Others hate it. There seems to be no middle ground. People are increasingly complaining about the state of the road verges and roundabouts. Some of these complaints are for practical reasons; allowing wild plants, grass and trees to grow taller obscures drivers' views at junctions. For others, the complaints are purely based on aesthetics; it just looks a mess.

This dislike of messy environments is not just local to where I live. I came across similar attitudes when visiting the city of Iquitos in Peru, a chaotic city of half a million people, double that of Milton Keynes, sitting on the banks of a tributary of the River Amazon in the middle of the jungle. Getting to Iquitos is not as easy as travelling to Milton Keynes. There are no roads connecting it to the rest of Peru. You either fly in or travel for several days along the river.

One day while there, we looked across the natural forest from a terrace in the city with our host Laure-Lee Lovering, a scientist working with BMS World Mission, specialising in environmental mission. From my perspective, considering the loss of so much natural forest along with the diversity of life for which it is home, it seemed valuable and worthy of preservation. Laura commented that many Peruvians disliked the messy wilderness. They were wary of its potential dangers (akin to that of the Israelites over the danger of the sea) and they preferred the forest to be tamed and ordered, shaped to human need and flourishing.

It seems that humans prefer order over disorder. In this, Peter Berger saw another sign of transcendence. Science brings order to the world on a universal scale. The universe is amazing and vast beyond imagination. Yet, in what is an infinitesimally small spec of the vast universe, it is mysterious that from seeing and ordering the everyday world and processes around us we find cosmic validity from the smallest to the largest scales of the cosmos. Order brings comfort and significance; it brings a sense of knowing, although undermined by the unknowing of the wonder of it all. Beyond this success at describing the physical nature of creation, there remains a feeling that this 'natural world… is not the only world, but only the foreground of another world in which love is not annihilated in death, in which therefore, the trust in the power of love to banish chaos is justified'.[47]

We come to the final stage in shaping the theological lens through which God might be found within the stunning imagery of science. Already we have shaped it by linking wonder with power, and playfulness with the diversity of life and forms found within the natural world. Completing the shaping, Bonaventure's vision of purpose, found within the love of God, is linked with the human desire for order.

The theme of order is a strong narrative of hope running through the Bible. The creation story begins with a description of divinely initiated creation as an unordered mess, a dark, storm-tossed ocean: 'In the beginning God created the heavens and the earth. Now the earth was formless and empty, darkness was over the surface of the deep, and the Spirit of God was hovering over the waters' (Genesis 1:1–2). To this, God brings order, separating sea, sky and land, filling all with myriad forms of life. Flowing from this original disordered ocean, throughout the Old Testament there is a fear of the sea. With Israel being a land-based nation, such fear is understandable. Yet beyond human fears, the image of the sea became a sign of the forces that opposed God within the world.

The Easter story also resonates with God bringing order to a messy world. In the incarnation, and most deeply in Jesus' crucifixion, God embraces the mess of the world, the forces that take away from God's purpose and life. The subsequent resurrection of Jesus declares the victory of God over disorder. This is a moment that points back to God beginning to bring order to the mess of the Earth's initial state in declaring, 'Let there be light' (Genesis 1:3).

It is tempting to link this statement with the scientific vision of the beginning of the universe in the Big Bang, where space and time, along with energy and matter, appear in a chaotic state. Yet, in reflecting upon the light of the first day of creation, Eastern Orthodox theologians have long distinguished between the revelation of divine being and physical light. As Richard Viladesau summarises: '"Let there be light" is not an optical phenomenon but the most shattering revelation of the face of God.'[48] John picks up this emphasis in the opening of his gospel in describing the coming of the Word, Jesus, into creation: 'The light shines in the darkness, and the darkness has not overcome it' (John 1:5).

The resurrection also points to the hope of new creation. Described within the final chapters of the Bible as 'a new heaven and a new earth', the new creation is a radical renewal: sin and disorder are banished – 'there was no longer any sea' – and the sun and moon are not needed to sustain it – 'for the glory of God gives it light, and the Lamb is its lamp' (Revelation 21: 1, 23). For Bonaventure, new creation and communion with God is the goal of the journey towards which all created beings are drawn. Things divinely created, displaying something of the imaginative creativity of God, are drawn in their pilgrimage by 'a profound love-born yearning, satisfied only [by]… loving union with God'.[49]

However, science provides a contrasting and differing vision of the future of the cosmos. Until 100 years ago, humanity's view of the history and size of the universe remained limited. Astronomer Edwin Hubble's work in the 1920s, measuring the distance and movement of galaxies, began to open the vista of a vast cosmos: a universe 93 billion light years across and containing over one hundred billion galaxies. Not a static cosmos, but one continually expanding from a moment of creation 13.7 billion years ago – the Big Bang – imagined originally by the Catholic priest and astronomer Georges Lemaître.

For many decades, it remained an open question to scientists whether the expansion would continue forever or whether the pull of gravity between the galaxies would eventually lead to contraction towards a 'Big Crunch'. This particular 'we don't know' was resolved in part by the discovery at the end of the 20th century that cosmic expansion was accelerating. Why? Well, again, 'we don't know'. It is attributed to the presence of a mysterious, poorly understood, repulsive 'dark energy', that appears to account for three quarters of the energy of the whole universe. In contrast, ordinary matter that makes up stars, planets and living beings accounts for only one twentieth of the energy of the universe. As the universe continues to expand, over billions of years, matter and energy will become too dispersed for new structures – including life – to emerge.[50] This is the so-called 'heat death' of the universe.

The difficulty of reconciling these two views of the final state of creation, its finis (ending) – one of decay and death, the other fullness of life and being – has led some renowned theologians of the late 20th century, such as Wolfhart Pannenberg, to wonder whether the descriptions 'relate to the same event'[51] – a theological 'we don't know!' However, other contemporary theologians, such Jürgen Moltmann and Keith Ward, suggest 'there is no need to think that the final state of the universe is the purpose for its existence'.[52] This puts our focus not on creation's finis but on its telos (purpose) – its goal expressed within its long pilgrimage.

For Bonaventure too, the purpose of creation was less about its finis than its telos of being drawn towards the love of God evidenced by its order and the connectivity of its diverse forms and life. Drawing upon classical ideas, still spoken of by scientists, Bonaventure saw beauty as pointing towards a loving creator. Indeed, science has found that much of nature is shaped by notions of symmetry, a facet often connected with human appreciation of beauty.

However, nature is not always classically beautiful. It is often found to be a turmoil of states of order and disorder – described as 'chaotic'. Nor from a Christian perspective is love always seemingly beautiful. The incarnation and death of Jesus on the cross are held to be the deepest expression of divine love: 'For God so loved the world that he gave his one and only Son' (John 3:16). Yet the physical suffering of Jesus on the cross, while expressed in beautiful depictions of art through Christian history aimed at inspiring worship and devotion, can hardly be said to be beautiful from a human perspective. Nor would the continual suffering of many people through history to the present day.

Scientifically, the term 'chaos' is suggestive of something more than the usual use of the word in common conversation or theological discussion. There it is often used negatively, to describe a state of disorder which, as Berger observes, humans resist. Yet, from a scientific perspective, a more positive position might be taken. Within science, 'chaos' describes the interplay of order and disorder that leads to unpredictability yet not total randomness.

Within the Christian imagination, God's love is expressed particularly in the death and resurrection of Jesus. This was an embracing of disorder and revelation in the hope of creation being drawn towards the order of God's eternal love. Science's view of a chaotic universe suggests that order arising out of disorder shapes the whole of history – past, present and future. John Polkinghorne, reflecting further on 'chaos', says, 'The creativity at the edge of chaos could be seen as a pale reflection' of the 'Trinitarian rhythm [of] sustaining [and] redeeming.'[53]

While the Christian notion of new creation remains hard to fully reconcile with scientific perspectives, nevertheless, through science's story of order emerging from disorder, God's love might be glimpsed. In this, science has revealed this vestige beyond Bonaventure's more limited vision of the world.

6

Divine windows

I was at a minister's conference some years ago organised by my local Baptist region. The topic was worship, and one session was on Greek Orthodox icons. This is not something you'd typically find as part of a Baptist worship service, but in my pilgrimage of faith I've found it good to explore alternative ways of worshipping and encountering God beyond your own tradition and practice. At the end, I asked a question: 'Can nature serve as an icon – a "divine window" through which God might be found?'

That question has expanded through the years to 'Can the imagery of science serve as an icon?' On our journey to this point, we have explored a way in which the scientific images might become a divine window, shaping a lens based upon wonder, playfulness and order. These are characteristics of science that enable the image to be captured. They are also experiences in life, in ways known and unknown, that draw us towards the presence of God.

Putting on spectacles with this prescription, in this chapter we will look through a series of scientific divine windows. These amazing images have been captured by humanity's scientific exploration of the cosmos and take us from the microscopic scales of life in the Earth's oceans out to the very edges of the cosmos.

In this journey into what science reveals of our world and cosmos, the activity and presence of God is assumed. The viewer is invited to share in a sacramental reading of the images, exploring a transcendental possibility of encountering the divine through them. Each image is accompanied by a written reflection shaped by the themes of wonder, playfulness and order. Icons and other religious imagery assume a familiarity with the narrative depicted by the image for them to be effective in fostering spiritual encounter and prayer, so a little of the science behind the image is told at a popular level.

In offering these written reflections, there is danger of restricting the sacramental imagination of the viewer. While the scientific story represented by the image remains the same for both myself as author and you as viewer, what I perceive through the image recorded in the written reflection may be different to what you might see. So, before reading the reflections, I encourage you to take some time to stay with the image. Ask yourself where you see the wonder, playfulness and order? What do these – and anything else about the picture – say to you about the nature, presence and action of God within the world and your life? The reflection may give you deeper insights, new things that you have not seen before. But then again, the wonder of the imagination is that you may see something different. That is the playfulness of the Spirit of the playful God!

The aim of this exercise is not only for you to gain new appreciation of this small set of images. The hope is that they will help you to learn a new way of seeing that will travel with you, allowing you to look for the presence, activity and being of God in the natural world around you. And the next time you watch one of those stunning science and nature documentaries that seem to have sent God to Coventry perhaps the divine will seem a little closer.

So, as we said at the start, come and join the journey, looking at the wonder of creation and for the wonder of the creator!

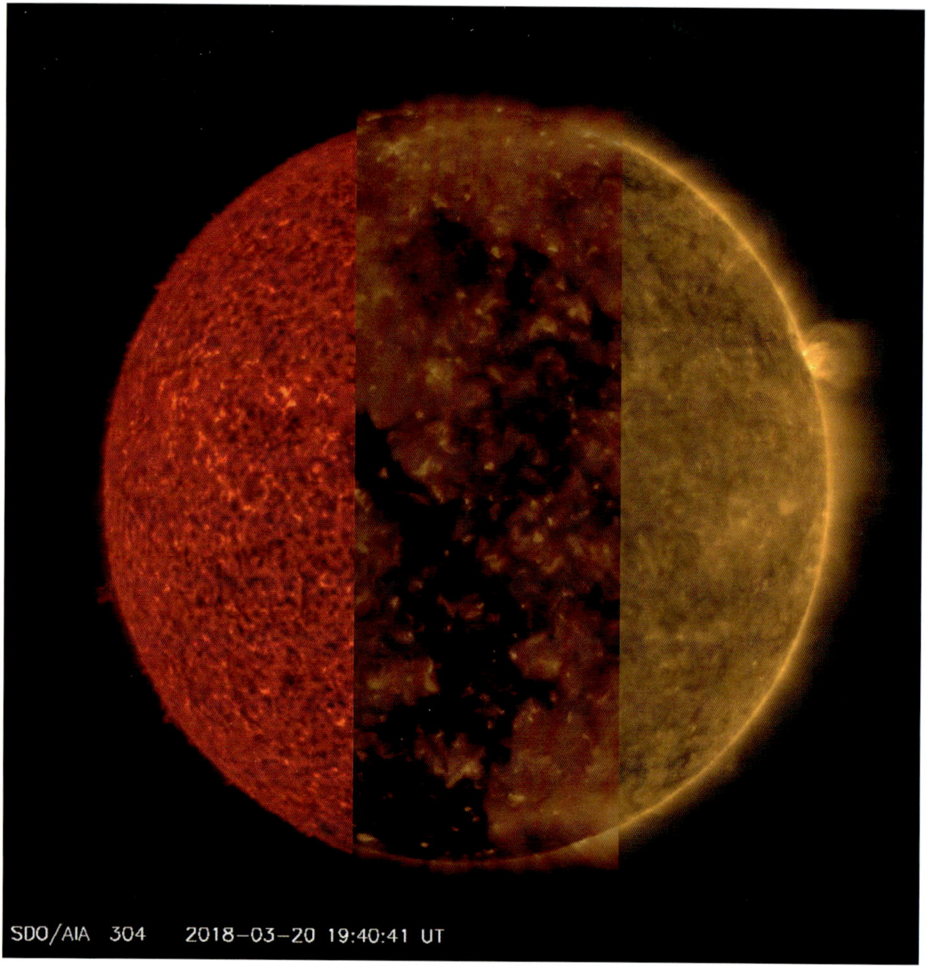

SDO/AIA 304   2018-03-20 19:40:41 UT

STAR

Image of the Sun taken by NASA Solar Dynamics Observatory in three different wavelengths of ultraviolet light.[54]

Star

In sacred art, a triptych is a painting comprising of three panes, each telling part of a story. They are a common form of medieval altar pieces and icons. This image is a triptych telling a story of the Sun beyond our natural sight. The picture playfully combines three images of the Sun taken in different wavelengths of light – not visible light, by which we see the world, but ultraviolet light. This light – whose wavelength is shorter than the familiar violet of the rainbow – is known through the painful experience of sunburn, and while it is invisible to our vision, here it comes into our sight through technology's gaze.

Since ancient times, the Sun has been humanity's constant yet mysterious companion. Many cultures saw the Sun as a divine being, a focus of worship. In contrast, the Jewish creation story casts the Sun among the created objects and beings of the world: 'God made… the [Sun] to govern the day… [and he] also made the stars' (Genesis 1:16).

In the fifth century BCE, the Greek philosopher Anaxagoras was the first recorded person to suggest that the Sun and stars were hot bodies, with the stars being far, far away. But few took him seriously. Two thousand years later, the Italian monk and Renaissance thinker Giordano Bruno also suggested the stars were like the Sun, with planets of their own inhabited by other beings. Condemned by both Catholics and Protestants, he was burnt at the stake in 1600. Was Bruno's death a sign of the struggle for truth between science and religion? More likely, it was down to his radical religious views rather than his novel scientific thinking.

It wasn't until the mid-19th century that clearer understanding was found. Scientists compared light from the Sun with those of the stars and found it to be similar. The Sun was like any other star, just a lot closer. It takes eight minutes for sunlight to travel to the Earth. Light from the next nearest star, Alpha Centauri in the southern hemisphere sky, takes just over four years.

The Sun remains an object of wonder and mystery, a powerful presence and symbol of divine power. Psalm 84:11 declares: 'For the Lord God is a sun and shield.' Just as the full blaze of the midday Sun is dangerous, John cautions of the mortal danger of gazing fully upon Christ's heavenly glory: 'His face was like the sun shining in all its brilliance… I fell at his feet as though dead' (Revelation 1:16–17).

Dangerous, yet at its rising and setting, the Sun's yellow light turns red as the other colours are scattered by gas molecules and dust in the atmosphere, its brilliance tempered by the smallest of things. This moment of wonder takes us beyond ourselves, bringing a sense of serenity and peace among the twists and turns of our lives, perhaps without knowing why. A mysterious moment, the touch of divine light is evoked by natural light – like the mystery of Jesus, through whom we see the divine life in bearable human form: 'the light of the world… the light of life' (John 8:12).

Like the paints of an artist's pallet, the Sun's overwhelming glow is a playful combination of different light: from X-rays through ultraviolet to the familiar visible colours of the rainbow and out to the heat of the infrared and radio waves beyond. Most of the light we see with our eyes comes from its surface layer, the photosphere. At 6,000 degrees centigrade, it's a playful, boiling cauldron of convection cells like those seen rolling in a saucepan or in the cloud fields scattered across the Earth. It contains rising plumes of gas, heat flowing from the million-degree furnace of nuclear fusion at the heart of the Sun.

Above this are even hotter, unseen layers, their mystery now being unwrapped through telescopes sent into space. The triptych image comes from the Solar Dynamics Observatory, orbiting beyond the Moon, constantly gazing sunward through the past decade and a half. On the left, in red, we see the chromosphere, the lowest layer of the Sun's atmosphere. Reaching up to 2,000 km above the surface, with temperatures rising to 50,000 degrees centigrade, ten times hotter than the surface. Like the surface layer of the Sun, its texture is moulded by convection cells, hotter, ascending regions appearing brighter. Spiracles penetrate up from the surface, giving the edge of the Sun a fuzzy appearance. These are hot flows of gas, associated with increases in the Sun's magnetic field. They are a 'we don't know' phenomena – wonder in search of scientific explanation.

In the middle is the corona. A layer of tenuous gas, it stretches out a million kilometres from the Sun, almost as wide as the Sun itself. Its blinding white light is wondrously revealed during a total solar eclipse as the Moon covers the face of the Sun. Its presence varies through the eleven-year cycle of the Sun between active and inactive phases. When the Sun is quiet, the corona is limited to a belt around the Sun's equator. When active it spreads across the polar regions, although the dark areas show holes where the Sun's magnetic field punches through causing streams of particles – the Solar Wind – to flow out across the Solar System, disrupting communication satellites around Earth.

While space telescopes allow us to see the corona constantly, rather than having to wait for a total eclipse, within the wonder, mystery remains. Temperatures rise within it to one million degrees centigrade. Science still puzzles over this process, which likely involves the swirls of hot gas seen at the edge of the right-hand pane of the solar triptych. Invisible magnetic lines of forces twist around the Sun as it rotates, breaking through the surface marked by loops of hot gas shooting above the surface, then cascading back down again.

The gentle Sun. A reassuring presence through human history. Bringing moments of wonder, serenity, along with unknowing. Unknowing revealed beyond our vision. A raging, playful turmoil of immense power; life-giving yet full of destructive power.

Without its warmth, life on Earth would not exist. Plants, on land and in the ocean, make use of its gentle light, forming sugars and oxygen from water and carbon dioxide. It provides the breath of life and food for other living creatures. And yet, the stream of ultraviolet light has the power to strip this away, scorching plants and causing mutations in DNA – life's foundation. This damage is averted by the Earth's natural sun block, the fragile ozone layer. Thirty kilometres high in the stratosphere, solar ultraviolet light transforms oxygen molecules into ozone,[55] reducing its intensity at the surface and thus protecting life.

This is a fragile balance. Fifty years ago, synthetic chemicals released into the atmosphere caused a thinning of the ozone layer above the south polar regions. The 1987 Montreal Protocol began to restrict their release. Nature continues to repair it today. Scientific understanding cautions us but also invites humanity to cooperate with God's creative imagination of the life-giving communion of Sun and Earth. To seek to live within the care of God, of which the psalmist's words remind us: 'The Lord watches over you – the Lord is your shade at your right hand' (Psalm 121:5).

MOON

Earthrise taken by astronaut Bill Anders of Apollo 8, Christmas Eve 1968.

Moon

The astronauts of Apollo 8 took this picture in a hurried moment on Christmas Eve 1968 as they became the first humans to orbit the Moon. Its imperfect framing, the Earth off centre above a sloping horizon, is evidence of an unanticipated moment of wonder akin to that evoked by a magnificent sunrise or the optical illusion of an overly large full Moon hanging low over the horizon. Named *Earthrise* on their return to Earth, only a few humans have seen this view; what was imagined through the ages is made real in human experience through the creativity of science and technology.

Blackness and shades of grey dominate, yet over the 'face of the deep' (Genesis 1:2, NRSV), the Earth shines out brightly. Beyond our natural vision and natural light, by which science reveals the wonder of the cosmos, it points towards the mystery of divine light, the source of wonder.

In the opening of his gospel, John speaks of the Word, Jesus, as one through whom 'all things were made; without him nothing was made that has been made' (John 1:3). *Earthrise* displays the rich playfulness of God in hues of blue, brown and green, hidden by the blinding whiteness of the clouds draped across the Earth. And woven amid this colourful vista are myriad forms of life beyond counting or imagining, of which humans are but one. In contrast, the Moon's shades of grey show a lifeless and sterile landscape, pale in comparison. Buzz Aldrin, the second human to walk on the Moon half a year later, in July 1969, described what he saw there as 'magnificent desolation'.[56] This phrase recalls another moment of magnificent desolation: Jesus crying out on the cross, 'My God, my God, why have you forsaken me?' (Matthew 27:46).

The rich Earth, rising brightly among blackness and over the Moon's desolation, suggests a memory of another rising 'at dawn on the first day of the week' (Matthew 28:1): Easter morning, when God the Father raised Jesus and revealed the hope of new life. The divine light 'shines in the darkness, and the darkness has not overcome it' (John 1:5).

Both Easter moments work together to bring forth Jesus' promise: 'I have come that they may have life, and have it to the full' (John 10:10). Likewise, the abundant Earth and the desolate Moon are vessels that bear divine goodness, symbols that in God 'all things work together for good' (Romans 8:28, see NIV footnote). Desolation and richness cooperate in bringing forth the purpose of God within creation. The barren Moon plays its part in enabling Earth's abundance. The orbital dance of Earth and Moon stabilises the wobble of the Earth's axis, reducing its climatic extremes. The Moon's gravitational pull on the Earth's oceans causes the twice daily tides shaping liminal coastal habitats, the cradle of life when it emerged from sea to land half a billion years ago.

From this long, fragile, painful pilgrimage of life, the human story arises. We are a being conscious not only of ourselves, but able to look out and around, to voice questions and understand the working of creation. Yet, we are silenced by the wonder and playfulness of it all, drawing us towards the divine agent behind and within it. We are creatures who, from among creation, are a symbol of hope, for God's intent is that 'creation itself will be liberated from its bondage to decay and brought into the freedom and glory of the children of God' (Romans 8:21).

Our very existence expresses the divine goal of creation: the fulfilment of creation's response to God. Our deep value is affirmed in the incarnation, when Jesus appears within the smallness of time and space, bearing the fullness of divine being in human life. This moment declares creation's inherent goodness, echoing across the Earth and its teaming creatures, to the magnificent desolation of the Moon and beyond.

Earth, small, alone, in the blackness of space above the barren Moon, might suggest otherwise, expressing the sheer hopelessness of a solely material universe devoid of divine presence. Yet, from *Earthrise* shines the light of God's continual work in drawing all things back to himself regardless of the seeming bleakness of existence. Imaginatively, it calls for a 'renewing of your mind. Then you will be able to test and approve what God's will is – his good, pleasing and perfect will' (Romans 12:2).

EARTH

Montage of images of the Earth taken by the US polar orbiting Suomi weather satellite, 23 January 2012.

Earth

From Earth, we can look up and see the wonder of a sky adorned with clouds. Now, with satellites that orbit our world, we gain new perspectives, previously only imagined. Search out a sci-fi movie from before the space age and look out for pictures of the Earth from space. It's an imagined world stripped bare of clouds, imagination that is laid bare by real images sent back from space of our home. This image too is a result of the human imagination. It's a collage of images taken by the Suomi weather satellite, a work of art arising from scientific and artistic creativity. The Suomi satellite travels from pole to pole every hundred minutes at a height of 800 km, giving a snapshot of the whole globe every day.

In the Bible, a friend advises the troubled Job:

> Stop and consider God's wonders.
> Do you know how God controls the clouds
>   and makes his lightning flash?
>
> **JOB 37:14–15**

Satellite images today are commonplace; they grace the weather forecasts that we see every day on our TVs and smart devices. In response, unlike Job, we might answer, 'Yes, we do know how the weather and clouds work.' But, while Job stopped and took in the wonder of it all, perhaps in our familiarity we fail to do the same. In fact, it's a wonder that we manage to predict the weather at all, matching our imagination to that of the creator of the clouds.

Measurements of temperature, wind and water from satellites have much improved the quality of our forecasts, together with bigger supercomputers and a fuller understanding of the processes with the atmosphere. Yet, our knowledge is never complete. The weather is chaotic. Small unknown details lead to substantial changes in possible futures. As Jesus said: 'The wind blows wherever it pleases. You hear its sound, but you cannot tell where it comes from or where it is going' (John 3:8). Perhaps along with Job we need to step back and consider the wonder of it all, bringing our creative imagination alongside the greater imagination of the creator.

Mirroring one another, both divine and human imagination are playful. Playful science enables understanding of the world and the construction of computers and satellites. The focus on their measurements and investigations are playful too. Clouds present an almost infinite variety of shape and texture. Trying to find one shaped the same as another is like finding the right piece in an ever-changing jigsaw. One day's fields of clouds lacing the globe will be different from the next as chaotic weather systems arise, live out their lives and die – to be replaced by new forms in their wake.

Around the equator, giant thunderstorms towering over 10–15 km high, reach upwards through the troposphere, the lowest layer of the Earth's atmosphere. Arising from a field of their smaller cousins, fair weather cumuli scattered over land and sea, bubbling up only a kilometre or so deep. Towering, powerful storms rising up, driven by the intense heat of the tropical sun warming land and oceans. Fast, tumbling streams of air move the sun's heat upwards, releasing more energy as water condenses and ice freezes around microscopic specks of salt and solid particles – dust, smoke, even condensed chemicals released by trees. As the flow of air slows, from their towering tops wispy, lace thin, ice clouds flow – angel wings embracing the world.

Further north and south, sheets of clouds stretch over entire oceans and continents. Marking the boundaries between warm and cold air, they swirl around weather systems that feed off the energy of the fast-moving rivers of air – jet streams – that meander around the globe closer to the poles. Slower upward movements play their part in moving the Sun's heat from the tropics towards more cooler climes. And along with heat, streams of water too.

One of the Psalms declares:

> [God] covers the sky with clouds;
> he supplies the earth with rain
> and makes grass grow on the hills.
>
> **PSALM 147:8**

A playful collection of clouds and movement, working together, plays its part to make the Earth a place where life might flourish. Clouds shine white because of the way their small droplets reflect the light of the Sun. It makes them seem solid, betraying their tenuous nature. Around half a percent of the Earth's atmosphere is water vapour. Only a minute proportion of this makes up the droplets of the clouds at any one time. Yet, from this small amount, comes the rain on which life depends. In one of his parables, Jesus talked of God's activity in the world being like 'the smallest of all seeds… Yet when planted, it grows and becomes the largest of all garden plants' (Mark 4:31–32). God begins with and values the small: a seed; a drop; a person.

Those who fly into space are often inspired to speak significant words that share their experience with the wider world. Neil Armstrong, the first human to step on the Moon in July 1969, said of that moment, 'That's one small step for man; one giant leap for mankind.' More recently, in another first, Jared Isaacman, the first non-government astronaut to take a walk in space during the September 2024 Polaris Dawn Space Flight, looked down upon the Earth and said, 'Back home, we have a lot of work to do, but from here – looks like a perfect world.'

This image is not one that you would see if you were orbiting above the Earth with them. Our planet spins on its axis every 24 hours as it travels around the Sun, changing from the brightness of day to the darkness of night. Yet, here, where is the night? Apart from the north pole, in its permanent winter darkness, the whole globe is bathed in glorious light. This is a trick of the creative way the image is artistically constructed, stitched from 13 orbits of the Suomi satellite, which follows a path that puts it over the equator at noon each pass.

We are left with an image of a world bathed in light, a perfect world in which night is banished. It is an icon that shines forth the hope of 'a new heaven and a new earth', which 'does not need the sun or the moon to shine on it, for the glory of God gives it light' (Revelation 21:1, 23). A world where God '"will wipe every tear from their eyes. There will be no more death" or mourning or crying or pain, for the old order of things has passed away' (Revelation 21:4). This is not yet our world, but it is a vision that God is working towards. This image invites us, small droplets though we may be, as the clouds reflect the light of the Sun, to shine with the hope of God bringing life.

AURORA

Aurora seen from the International Space Station, 11 August 2024.

Aurora

It's a warm summer's evening in 2024, rare in England despite much of the Earth baking under the increasing heat of a changing climate. As the day fades and the night begins, we watch for streaks of light arching across the sky. Shooting stars: small grains of space dust colliding with the atmosphere at colossal speeds. The Perseid meteor shower is a regular feature of the August night sky. It is a stream of debris left by the comet Swift-Tuttle on its century-long orbit around the Sun. Space dust, long in darkness, briefly shining forth in fiery oblivion. Patiently watching, our attention is distracted. The darkening northern sky begins to glow in faint hues of green and pink, stretching across the horizon. There are towering columns of light, flicking, fading, returning. On the edge of sight, solidified by the cameras of our mobile phones, is an auroral display, rare so far south. It feels like a moment of blessing and grace. It is fleeting compared to the annual Perseids, but our wonder is intensified by the chance of time and place.

An ancient song in the Bible says, 'The heavens declare the glory of God; the skies proclaim the work of his hands' (Psalm 19:1). Living closer to the equator, the writer may never have seen an aurora gracing and dancing across the sky.

This is also true for many today, and as a result, seeing the aurora is one of the world's bucket list of wonders that people chase across the globe. Yet, as we look up, so others chasing across the world look down.

From space, as the International Space Station sweeps around the globe every 90 minutes, at a height of 250 km, the aurora can be a common sight. This image is one taken by astronauts looking down as we were looking up. Of such a view, one astronaut, Jasmin Moghbeli, shares: 'I love it… every time I look out the window, I'm in awe… amazed at how alive and beautiful our planet is.'[57]

An aurora is a mesmerising display of creation's artistry. It is brought to life by the interplay of invisible charged subatomic particles flowing from the Sun, shaped by the brush strokes of the Earth's magnetic field, bringing alive the tenuous upper atmosphere of the Earth. Channelled towards the polar regions, the charged solar wind spirals along invisible lines of magnetic force. It crashes into the faint, invisible atmosphere of the Earth hundreds of kilometres high. Oxygen glows green, while energised nitrogen shines pink, in a dancing display of the play of the Earth's magnetic field. Folding and twisting, the magnetic field responds to its partner's – the solar wind's – own twists and turns. Matter and energy flow along magnetic field lines reaching out from the very core of the Earth to the edge of space, connecting Earth and heaven. Invisible force made visible.

Wonder invites us to explore the hidden mysteries of the universe. Science enables humanity to appreciate and play alongside God's imagination and creativity. Creation is mysteriously shaped by Jesus, in whom 'all things were created… in heaven and on earth, visible and invisible… and in him all things hold together' (Colossians 1:16–17), the one who steps into creation, 'the image of the invisible God', making 'him known' (Colossians 1:15; John 1:18).

Jesus connects heaven and earth. He is a sign of the love of God for people and all creatures in the community of the Earth. It is often said that life on Earth is possible because its orbits the Sun in the Goldilocks zone: not too hot, not too cold, but just right. Yet alone this is insufficient. As with the aurora, a communion of interconnected forces play their part. The Moon stabilises the wobble of the spinning Earth, moderating natural shifts in climate. A just-right atmosphere warms the Earth, and its invisible magnetic field traps, channels and diverts the raw radiation of the Sun, which would damage and limit the potential of the Earth to bear life.

The invisible made visible, the aurora points not only to the interwoven artistry of God but enables us 'to grasp how wide and long and high and deep is the love of Christ' (Ephesians 3:18) for creation. God enables a world like ours to emerge and thrive among the chaos of it all. It is an invitation too for us to reflect upon our role in sharing God's purpose in our lives. The aurora, a sign of the glory of God, shines divine love across the globe and reminds us of Jesus' invitation to 'shine before others, that they may see your good deeds and glorify your Father in heaven' (Matthew 5:16).

DUST

Image taken by Suomi weather satellite, across the equatorial Atlantic from Africa towards the Americas, 25 June 2014, showing a river of Saharan dust.

Dust

This satellite image is a vista that few have seen with their own eyes. Now, through technologically enhanced vision, it is one that all might share.

Job was encouraged to look up at the sky by his friend Elihu, to 'stop and consider God's wonders' (Job 37:14). To look up and consider how:

> The drops of water,
> > which distil as rain to the streams;
> the clouds pour down their moisture
> > and abundant showers fall on mankind.
> Who can understand how he spreads out the clouds,
> > how he thunders from his pavilion?
>
> **JOB 36:27–29**

So, looking down, what do you see? What catches your eye?

At the bottom, we see the brown, dry Sahara, transitioning gradually through the Sahel to the lush forests of the lands of equatorial Africa. A line of thunderstorms flows from their verdant lands, driven by the heat of sun-drenched moist land and warm ocean waters, towering 10–15 km tall. Such storms traversed continents and oceans long before humans made their epic journeys of discovery around the globe.

In the middle, we see the lines of smaller, low, fair-weather cumuli that track the flow of the gentle trade wind. Look more closely still, at the bottom right, and there are hints of waves in the air, marked by long cloud streets, as the wind flows around the Canary Islands.

In the distance, hidden by the curvature of the Earth, is the forest of the Amazon, covered in clouds which provide abundant water sustaining its lush canopy. And on to edge of the Earth, there is a thin blue band. It is strange to think all the movement and energy marked by the clouds is contained in a thin layer of air coating the vastness of the Earth – as thin as the peel around an apple.

So, again. What did you see? What caught your eye?

This is a view Job never had. Perhaps it takes a God's-eye view of looking down to appreciate fully the wonders of God. Yet, Job responded: 'My ears had heard of you but now my eyes have seen you' (Job 42:5). Such a response asks a question of a generation with a bigger, broader and higher view of the world.

What did you see? What caught your eye? In the wonder of it all, did you glimpse divine power, majesty and handiwork?

Look again. Our eyes are often drawn to the impressive magnificence of the vast and large, the seemingly important. And yet, perhaps we have missed something. What is that brown smudge spoiling the pristine white of the clouds and the turquoise blue of tropical oceans? With our image enhancing apps on our cameras we might clean up the image. Yet, take it away, and the playful wonder that you see will be lost.

This smudge is a stream of dust flowing across the ocean from the dry Sahara, paralleling the clouds flowing from moister but not hotter climes further south. Grains of sand, picked up by the whirling winds of dust devils, found not only on Earth but across the red deserts of Mars too, are lifted high into the sky, to be blown by rivers of air across the tropical ocean and up into higher latitudes. The dust mixes with storm systems, turning the sky yellow and orange – cars too as it falls in the rain, leaving that annoying coating of dust.

Yet, without dust, the lace covering of clouds would be thinner, patchier. Water vapour would struggle to condense into droplets alone. Cloud condensation nuclei quicken the process. Small particles collect molecules of water vapour together, enabling droplets of water and ice crystals to form. Salt from the oceans; volcanic dust; smoke from human and forest fires; pollution from factories; Saharan dust – these enable the playful patterns of the clouds which catch our eyes.

God's play within creation begins not with the large, but with the small. From small, insignificant particles come life-giving water, sustaining the life of the world. And from dust comes life. The Bible's creation story speaks of life beginning from dust: 'God formed a man from the dust of the ground and breathed into his nostrils the breath of life, and the man became a living being' (Genesis 2:7). This first human, Adam, is a spiritual being capable of connecting with God yet also connected to the very stuff of the Earth. He, along with Eve, is nourished by the fruit of dust, fed by rain: 'mist came up from the earth and watered the whole surface of the ground… all kinds of trees [grew] out of the ground – trees that were pleasing to the eye and good for food' (Genesis 2:6, 9, see NIV footnote).

Dust still plays its part in sustaining the life of the Earth, not only in watering it, but in feeding the soil on which plants depend. In the verdant tropical forest of the Amazon, intense rainfall quickly washes out rich nutrients that cause plants and trees to flourish. These are replenished as dust blown across oceans falls to the ground, bringing phosphorus, iron and other chemicals needed for plants to thrive.

This helps create and sustain a natural garden, beautiful to see and good for food – a sign of God's playful creativity and provision for life. This is something that we can forget as we strive to re-shape the world to meet our needs for food, energy and material for our technology. Our activities can turn verdant forest and landscape to dust. The overgrazing of pasture at the edge of deserts by our flocks and herds can turn them to arid wastelands. Global warming caused by pumping increasing amounts of greenhouse gases into the atmosphere shifts weather systems, leaving once fertile lands parched. To make space for our cattle, verdant forests are felled to be replaced by grassland, displacing people and other living beings that called them home. If we are not careful, we can disturb the complex balances of the world that enable its fullness.

In the Psalms, a writer praises God, recognising that they are 'fearfully and wonderfully made' (Psalm 139:14). Through the creativity of science, revealing the communion of big and small, the same might be said of the whole Earth. Each part, big and small, plays a role, interwoven with divine purpose. And made from the dust, we are reminded how our lives are deeply woven with the very fabric and life of the Earth and within the life and purpose of God.

So, look again. What did you see? What caught your eye?

In the wonder of it all, did you glimpse divine power, majesty and handiwork? And seeing this, what might you do to share in God's purpose to bring life to the Earth?

LIFE

Phytoplankton bloom in the waters around Gotland, a Swedish island in the Baltic Sea, 13 June 2005.

Life

This image blurs the boundary of art and science, as do many of the stunning scientific images that we see scattered across media. The raw data collected by a satellite is transformed through creative image processing, enhanced colours drawing out hidden structures. Here, the colour palette of vibrant blues and greens evoke remembrance of the swirling brush strokes of a Van Gogh masterpiece, combining both scientific and artistic imagination.

Looking down upon the Swedish island of Gotland, wonder is found in the surrounding Baltic Sea. We see a phytoplankton bloom: billions of microscopic plants, tracing out the flow and whirls of tides and currents within the ocean. They create patterns like those seen in clouds flowing with the wind in the atmosphere above. Water and air are both shaped by the same complex equations which reveal divine artistry.

The upwelling of nutrients from the dark deep ocean feeds an eruption of vibrant life. Desert dust too, carried across oceans, feeds the sunlit surface waters, bringing the gift of life. These micro-organisms are the base of the oceanic food chain, sustaining even the largest of creatures, the blue whale.

Before science's vision gave us such vibrant images and deeper understanding, the ancients appreciated the wondrous playfulness of the oceans:

> How many are your works, Lord!
>   In wisdom you made them all;
>   the earth is full of your creatures.
> There is the sea, vast and spacious,
>   teeming with creatures beyond number –
>   living things both large and small.
> There the ships go to and fro,
>   and Leviathan, which you formed to frolic there.
>
> **PSALM 104:24–26**

The writer of these words was as acute an observer of the world as scientists are today. They too marvelled at whales dancing through the waves, playfully twisting in the air. They saw the creativity of God in the variety of creatures that swim in the seas. Their praise would have deepened if only they could have glimpsed the seeming infinite variety of shape and form of the phytoplankton seen through modern microscopes, revealing intricacies of divine playfulness emerging from evolution's game, exploring the seemingly never-ending possibilities of playful DNA's fluidity, flexibility. Yet, is our praise nourished by such playful wonder? Or diminished by our deeper scientific knowledge?

While the community of the plankton is visible from orbit, the presence of the larger creatures is harder to see. Drawn to graze on the abundant plankton, they are a drop in the ocean compared to their small brethren. Scientists estimate that up to 80% of the mass of life in the ocean lie within the community of these smallest of creatures. Certainly, 'How many are your works, Lord! In wisdom you made them all.'

In the story of the Bible, the sea is not always depicted as life-giving. Written by a land-dwelling culture, the Bible presents the sea as a place to be feared and as a symbol of all that opposed God and took away from life. Such imagery draws from the opening lines of the Bible's creation story:

> In the beginning God created the heavens and the earth. Now the earth was formless and empty, darkness was over the surface of the deep, and the Spirit of God was hovering over the waters.
> **GENESIS 1:1–2**

The swirling patterns marked out by the green chlorophyll of plankton capture the disorder of those lifeless beginnings. As the Spirit of God was poised to bring forth life then, so from within this tumbling and turning comes the breath of life. Not only is life within the oceans sustained by these small creatures, but the whole community of life across the Earth. Using the light of the Sun, these tiny plants are responsible for maintaining half the oxygen in the atmosphere – twice as much as the rainforests whose preservation is of so much concern as we become increasingly aware of the damage humans are causing to the planet. Like their forest cousins, phytoplankton too play a vital role within the climate system, drawing down into the oceans a third of the carbon dioxide that human society produces, slowing its growth within the atmosphere, moderating the impact of climate change.

The swirling, glistening phytoplankton speak of the wisdom of God in his love for creation. Yet, while they bring life, death is present too. Living in the surface layers of the ocean, algal blooms block light from penetrating deeper, starving other plants of energy. And as they die, their decay depletes the surface waters of oxygen, limiting the life of animals drawn to feed on them.

The interplay of life and death has long been woven into these creatures' pilgrimage. Two billion years ago, when the world was half as old as it was today, their ancestors first learned to harness the light of the Sun to enable life. Turning the Earth green, creatures appeared that used chlorophyll to turn carbon dioxide and sunlight to sugar for energy, releasing oxygen in the process. Slowly, over millions of years, oxygen grew in the atmosphere. This is life-giving for us and other creatures today, yet it was poison to earlier forms of life, bringing extinction (although some hang on in the dark deeper depths of the ocean devoid of oxygen). This life was as equally wondrous, playful and interwoven as that we find today, equally precious to God and a part of divine purpose.

While the words of Psalm 104 celebrate the playful exuberance of life, big and small, which is a sign of God's wisdom, there is a recognition that within its flow there are endings as well as beginnings:

> When you take away their breath,
>   they die and return to the dust.
> When you send your Spirit,
>   they are created,
>   and you renew the face of the ground.
>
> **PSALM 104:29–30**

While such beginnings and endings have been known of old, science raises new possibilities and questions. Within the chaos of the world, while there is a raising to order, a falling to disorder remains. Through the long pilgrimage of life on the Earth, there has been five or six endings of life. At times over 90% of species have been lost to extinction. How is this to be understood within the purpose of a God who declares creation good, amplified by the divine coming to live as a created being in Jesus? A God whose being is defined by love?

God's love is neither distant nor inactive. It is active and embracing of all things. In stepping into creation, Jesus comes to 'reconcile to himself all things… by making peace through his blood, shed on the cross' (Colossians 1:20). He is the one through whom all things were made, and he embraces the disorder of death. Yet, the 'Spirit of [God]… raised Jesus from the dead' (Romans 8:11). And that same Spirit continues to be creatively active within the life of the world, resisting disorder, sustaining and bringing forth new life.

While questions linger, perhaps in this image we glimpse something of the love of God: divine love that calls to us through wonder and is expressed within the wild and overflowing diversity and bounty of the world. This love is present even in the beginnings and endings of its smallest creatures caught up in the twisting and turning of currents beyond their understanding and control. This divine love is also present amid the twisting and turnings, and within the beginnings and endings, of our own lives.

OTHER WORLDS

Composite panorama of the Paraitepuy Pass in Gale Crator captured by the Curiosity Mars rover, 8 April 2023.

Other worlds

In musical pieces, the *cantus firmus* is a repeating, often bass, tune, a foundation on which other parts of the melody are overlaid. In Genesis, the repeated phrase 'And there was evening, and there was morning' (1:5) provides a *cantus firmus* for the interwoven notes of the symphony of the Bible's creation story. More than a statement of the daily passing of night and day as the Earth spins, it is a declaration of certainty of God's faithfulness.

In the days of exile in Babylon, when to the Jewish people life appeared to have returned to the days of formlessness and emptiness at the beginning of the story, the prophet Jeremiah spoke God's words of hope:

> This is what the Lord says: 'If I have not made my covenant with day and night and established the laws of heaven and earth, then I will reject the descendants of… Abraham, Isaac and Jacob. For I will restore their fortunes and have compassion on them.'
>
> **JEREMIAH 33:25–26**

Sunrise and sunset are often moments of serenity amid a turbulent world, marking the continued creative activity of God to bring order and life. The powerful Sun speaks of the greatness and glory of God, as well as God's faithful care. As the writer of Lamentations says:

> Because of the Lord's great love we are not consumed,
>   for his compassions never fail.
> They are new every morning;
>   great is your faithfulness.
> **LAMENTATIONS 3:22–23**

Science gives a view of creation beyond our usual human perspective. Earthrise seen from the Moon is one such view. Yet, here is a view that no person has experienced first-hand: sunrise and sunset over Mars.

This image was taken as the Curiosity rover slowly trundled across the surface of Mars. This rover is one of many probes that have orbited the planet and landed upon its surface over the past 60 years. The image is an imaginative combination of two views of the same scene looking back upon its path marked in the sand through Paraitepuy Pass in Gale Crater, looking back across hills to the crater wall and beyond to distant mountains, 50 km away.

One image was taken early in the morning; the other later in the evening of the same day. They have been imaginatively spliced together and coloured to capture the wonder of the two moments.

Shining red in the night sky, Mars was well known to Earth's ancient peoples. Its colour led to association with war, its imagined inhabitants threatening the Earth in H.G. Wells' *War of the Worlds*. Yet, until visited by space probes, its true nature remained much of a mystery.

The creation story describes the original state of creation as 'formless and empty' (Genesis 1:2). In Hebrew, it literally means a trackless desert or a desert without water, a description that aptly describes the surface of Mars. It is an ancient landscape, a stony, rocky desert, coloured red by iron oxide – rust – within the sand. Different, yet strangely familiar to human eyes, like the rocky deserts found on Earth or a beach scene, sand cracked by the drying Sun as the tide recedes. You could imagine children joyfully building sandcastles or turning over the rocks, like the rover, curiously looking for what surprises lie underneath.

Yet, among this emptiness lies stunning wonder equal, even greater, to that of the Earth, such as Olympus Mons, an ancient volcano more than twice as high as Mount Everest. Or the Valles Marineris, a canyon 4,000 km long, dwarfing North America's Grand Canyon. Among Mars' battered, cratered surface, reminiscent of the Moon's, lie hints of the presence of water: in its polar caps; in clouds within its thin atmosphere; frozen deep under its surface.

And carved into its landscape are hints of a warmer, hopeful past: of flowing rivers, lakes and seas – water stripped away through long ages as the solar wind ravaged Mars' atmosphere, unprotected by a strong magnetic field. And perhaps too, life lost with it.

From the perspective of faith, it can be hard to fathom and appreciate God's wisdom within the long history of the playful, vast wonder of the cosmos. Despite such barrenness, sunset and sunrise silently speak of the enduring, embracing faithfulness of God beyond our imagining. And, alongside this steady bass tone, a dynamic, playful tune is also heard in the song of creation. 'The Spirit of God was hovering' (Genesis 1:2) – literally vibrating – over creation.

In musical composition, the technique of vibrato – a rapid variation in pitch of notes – is used to evoke emotion from within the music. Robotic rovers on Mars, along with witnessing the steady *cantus firmus* of sunrise and sunset, have recorded the sound of the wind flowing across the valleys, hills and craters of the barren landscape. If we could stand alongside the rover, we might hear in the wind the love of God that calls forth and embraces all that has been made: the Spirit's vibrating over the trackless desert of creation.

The trackless desert calls to us. There is talk of sending not only robots to Mars, but humans too. Is this sending out of life, bringing life to a barren world, a response to the call of God's Spirit over creation, bringing forth its potential?

Or is it merely the hubris of humanity, unsatisfied with shaping and breaking our world, looking to shape another in a better way?

The image of the love of the vibrating Spirit over barren creation resonates with another divine sending and giving. For God so loved the cosmos that he gave his one and only Son (John 3:16), for 'through him all things were made' (John 1:3). The Son was given to bring love and life to emptiness, of places and of life. And through the given one, the playful tune of the Spirit gives new life to creatures able to share in the playful love of God: 'Peace be with you! As the Father has sent me, I am sending you… Receive the Holy Spirit' (John 20:21–22).

The sights and sounds of Mars speak more deeply to us than to our sense of playful adventure alone. And closer to home on Earth, we are invited to be open to fulfilling the potential that God places within the cosmos, and within creatures such as us. We are invited to share in bringing divine love and life to barren lives and places – our own, and others, near and far.

COSMOS

James Webb Space Telescope, First Deep Field, Galaxy Cluster SMACS 0723.

Cosmos

The James Webb Space Telescope, with its 6.5 m wide mirror, hangs in the coldness of space beyond the orbit of the Moon. It looks out across the vast universe for light which our eyes cannot see: infrared light or heat energy. Its Deep Field image captures the vastness of the cosmos. 'Deep' in time, it can picture the universe in its infant years, one billion years after the Big Bang. Yet the portion of the universe pictured is hardly a 'field'. That suggests a large open space, while this image is but a pin prick of the night sky, the size of a grain of sand picked up from a field held out at arm's length.

Behind the foreground of stars, a myriad of bright objects are scattered. These are galaxies, swirling masses of hundreds of millions of stars. In the centre lies the SMACS 0723 cluster of galaxies. As Adam named the animals, so science continues the game, though perhaps not as imaginatively. SMACS 0723 is found within the more imaginatively named constellation of Volans, the flying fish, in the southern hemisphere night sky. Lying 4.6 billion light years away, light from these galaxies began travelling towards the telescope at the time the Sun and its planets were forming from a cloud of swirling dust and gas.

The image reveals thousands of galaxies invisible to our naked eyes. Yet, within it, still older ones are to be found, invisible both to our eyes and even to the huge mirror of the James Webb without an additional lens. The gravity of SMACS 0723 bends, distorts and magnifies the light of galaxies three times as distant – some up to 13 billion light years away. Seen as the bright streaks of reddish light that circle the centre of the image, they are turned red by the expansion of the universe that shifts their light to longer wavelengths away from their true colour.

In the Bible, God's challenge to Abram was to 'look up at the sky and count the stars – if indeed you can count them' (Genesis 15:5). While science allows us to count the vast numbers of stars within the cosmos, like Abram, the wonder of them all remains beyond human knowing and imagining.

The psalmist writes:

> The heavens are telling the glory of God,
>   and the firmament proclaims his handiwork.
> Day to day pours forth speech,
>   and night to night declares knowledge.

> There is no speech, nor are there words;
> > their voice is not heard;
> yet their voice goes out through all the earth,
> > and their words to the end of the world.
>
> **PSALM 19:1–4 (NRSV)**

A silent voice of praise passes through the creation to the creator, through whose word the universe is created. The James Webb image both shows the power of the creator along with the terror of smallness in the face of a vast universe. It invites a response of humble praise, by which the human voice makes the louder, silent praise of the cosmos audible.

Children often express playful delight at the immense number of stars and galaxies that the image reveals. Divine playfulness is found in the variety of shapes and colours the galaxies exhibit. As with Adam, the dance of divine and human playfulness continues to entwine in the playfulness of science. In the early 20th century, Edwin Hubble named the galaxies according to their morphology: spiral, elliptical, irregular. Still, such ordering fails to capture individual uniqueness, for not one galaxy is identical to another.

Seemingly infinite individuality within vastness may deepen feelings of being lost or alone. Yet the divine voice that shapes all things is one that:

> Heals the brokenhearted
> and binds up their wounds.
> He determines the number of the stars;
> he gives to all of them their names.
> Great is our Lord and abundant in power;
> his understanding is beyond measure.
>
> **PSALM 147:3–5 (NRSV)**

Our eyes are drawn to the light within creation. Light recalls the divine 'light [that] shines in the darkness' (John 1:5) drawing creation towards fulfilment. Yet, darkness too plays its part. Mysterious dark matter binds stars into galaxies and draws galaxies into clusters, painting their pattern across space. While neither emitting nor absorbing light, dark matter's presence is felt through the pull of its gravity that even bends the path of light. It is a hidden presence echoing the hidden divine presence that shapes and sustains, and in whom 'all things hold together' (Colossians 1:17).

God's purpose is 'to reconcile to himself all things, whether things on earth or things in heaven, by making peace through his blood, shed on the cross' (Colossians 1:20). Jesus' death embraces the disorder of creation, his resurrection taming it towards a new order – chaotic redemption. Yet, scientific understanding seemingly clashes with this hope.

While dark matter binds galaxies together, an unknown dark energy pushes them apart. The ever-expanding cosmos races towards the time when the light of the stars will dim, and galaxies will be smeared out as the universe expands towards a cold darkness. The tendency to disorder will overcome the struggle towards order. Is this the death of hope? Sweet praise, turned to a scream of despair? Darkness eclipsing even divine light?

The psalmist writes:

> If I say, 'Surely the darkness shall cover me,
>   and night wraps itself around me,'
> even the darkness is not dark to you;
>   the night is as bright as the day,
>   for darkness is as light to you.
>
> **PSALM 139:11–12 (NRSV)**

These ancient words suggest hope for a future far more distant from us than we are from the psalmist. God is not limited by our material sense of the world. Even at the end, when darkness dims light below human perception, even beyond the giant telescopes of our playful creativity, God might still perceive hope and purpose.

Yet perhaps divine hope is not to be found in this far future moment of which our scientific understanding catches a glimpse, but in the journey of creation and life itself. This journey is woven within the being of God, for as Paul writes, 'we live and move and have our being' (Acts 17:28). Divine hope shines in the darkness through the silent praise of myriads of galaxies. Galaxies shaped by redeeming chaos bringing forth within them stars, planets and life – even conscious life that expresses divine purpose by its imaginative creativity and curiosity over the material and spiritual world; beings who express divine purpose through growth in their sense of community with one another and the life of the Earth and the cosmos. Perhaps the embodiment of divine purpose is not found at the end, nor in the vastness of space and time, but through the journey of human lives, seeking signs of the divine light woven among our everyday worlds.

Epilogue: gazing with God

My early pilgrimage through life led me to send God to Coventry – which is not far from the city of Leicester, where I went in my late teens to study physcis and astrophysics, seeking to satisfy my curiosity as to how the universe ticked. Over a couple of years, discovering the way the universe was ordered and connected, seeing the wonderful images of planets, stars and galaxies revealed through new telescopes and space probes, as well as spending time look through the telescope at the university observatory, I began to wonder. One morning, walking down familiar streets on the way to the day's lectures, an unfamiliar thought came to mind. What if there is a God behind it all?

I was unaware these experiences were close to Bonaventure's vestiges or Peter Berger's signals of transcendence. Even back then, they spoke of the possibility of nature and the images of science acting as an icon. They were divine windows through which God might be encountered and known. And if that is true of my own experience of life and science, it may be the same for others too.

Since then, science has grown in its ability to capture amazing images of the universe, from its smallest scales out to the very edges and beginning of the cosmos. In a world awash with visual media, God calls to us through the wonder, playfulness and order of it all.

In sharing this journey, I hope you have grown in your appreciation of science and what it reveals of the amazing universe and world, which is a gift to small creatures such as us. We can look up, out and down, creatively exploring and comprehending from our small part of the universe something of where it has come from and where it is going. In all the wonders we have encountered, this is the most wondrous and puzzling thing of all: that we are creatures who can connect our experiences of a connected universe, piecing together its and our story.

At the start of this journey, for some readers God might have been sent to Coventry. For others, it might not be God but science that ended up there. My hope is that you have discovered a fresh appreciation of both, finding a way to allow science and faith to speak together – even allowing God to speak through them, drawing you closer, allowing God to be present to your life, and you present to God. My hope is that you will be more open to the chaotic love of God found in Jesus' life, death and resurrection, that you will see the world in a new way, through a new pair of glasses. I hope you too will discover that 'in [God] we live and move and have our being' (Acts 17:28).

So, as was said at the end of the first chapter, we say again at the end: come and join the journey, looking at the wonder of creation and for the wonder of the creator!

Notes

1. Peter L. Berger, *A Rumour of Angels: Modern society and the rediscovery of the supernatural* (Anchor, 1970), p. 5.
2. Timothy Radcliffe, *Alive in God: A Christian imagination* (Bloomsbury Continuum, 2019), p. 2.
3. Berger, *A Rumour of Angels*, p. 70.
4. A book was published to accompany the display – Neil MacGregor, *Living with the Gods: On beliefs and peoples* (Allen Lane, 2018).
5. Berger, *A Rumour of Angels*, p. 31.
6. Charles Taylor, *A Secular Age* (Harvard University Press, 2007), p. 98. 'Disenchantment' is a term that Taylor borrows from the German sociologist Max Weber.
7. The shift from 'signs and symbols' to 'concepts and mechanism' as a theological focus began during the 13th and 14th centuries within the western church, from what is called 'exemplarism' towards 'nominalism'. Ironically, it was led in part by thinkers such as Robert Grosseteste, Roger Bacon and William of Ockham, members of the Franciscan order whose theological origin drew heavily upon exemplarism and the sacramental imagination.
8. Tony Jones, *The Sacred Way: Spiritual practices for everyday life* (Zondervan, 2005), p. 103.
9. David Brown and Ann Loades (eds), *The Sense of the Sacramental: Movement and measure in art and music, place and time* (SPCK, 1995), p. 9.

10 Cheryl Forbes, *Imagination: Embracing a theology of wonder* (Multnomah Press, 1986), p. 55; Charles Harold Dodd, *The Parables of the Kingdom* (Nisbet, 1936), p. 16.
11 Michael Benson, *Other Worlds: Visions of our solar system* (Natural History Museum, 2017), pp. 10–11. This book, published to accompany the exhibit, contains many small-scale images from the display.
12 Siân Ede, *Art and Science* (I.B. Tauris, 2005), p. 187.
13 Paul Evdokimov, *The Art of the Icon: A theology of beauty* (Oakwood Publications, 1990), p. 100.
14 James Forest, *Praying with Icons* (Orbis, 1997), p. 30. Commenting upon the ability of creation to evoke an experience of awe and wonder, Forest suggests that akin to the experience of praying with icons, 'to glimpse the vastness of the cosmos [is] to become more aware of the hidden structures of [divine] being.'
15 Zachary Hayes, *The Gift of Being: A theology of creation* (Liturgical Press, 2001), p. 67.
16 Cheslyn Jones, Geoffrey Wainwright, Edward Yarnold (eds), *The Study of Spirituality* (SPCK, 1986), p. 189.
17 Ewert Cousins (ed.), *Bonaventure: The Soul's Journey into God, The Tree of Life, The Life of St Francis* (Paulist Press, 1978), p. 67.
18 Zachary Hayes, *Bonaventure: Mystical writings* (Tau Publishing, 1999), p. 978.
19 Ede, *Art and Science*, p. 1.
20 Garrett Green, *Imagining God: Theology and the religious imagination* (Eerdmans, 1998), pp. 43, 70.
21 Radcliffe, *Alive in God*, p. 5.
22 Karl Rahner, *Theological Investigations*, Vol. 23, Joseph Donceel and Hugh M. Riley (trans) (The Crossroad Publishing Company, 1992), p. 158.
23 Forbes, *Imagination*, pp. 18, 39.
24 Michael Polanyi and Harry Prosch, *Meaning* (University of Chicago Press, 1977), p. 83.
25 Polanyi and Prosch, *Meaning*, p. 101.

26 Richard Viladesau, *Theological Aesthetics: God in imagination, beauty and art* (Oxford University Press, 1999), p. 149.
27 Polanyi and Prosch, *Meaning*, p. 64.
28 Polanyi and Prosch, *Meaning*, pp. 97–99.
29 Thomas S. Kuhn, *The Structure of Scientific Revolutions* (University of Chicago Press, 1970), p. 10.
30 Polanyi and Prosch, *Meaning*, p. 101.
31 Celia Deane-Drummond, *Wonder and Wisdom: Conversations in science, spirituality and theology* (Darton, Longman and Todd, 2006), p. 31.
32 Richard Dawkins, *Unweaving the Rainbow: Science, delusion and the appetite for wonder* (Faber and Faber, 1997), p. 17.
33 Deane-Drummond, *Wonder and Wisdom*, p. 142.
34 Michael Mayne, *This Sunrise of Wonder: Letters for the journey* (Fount, 1995), p. 84.
35 Deane-Drummond, *Wonder and Wisdom*, p. 133.
36 John Macquarrie, *A Guide to the Sacraments* (SCM, 1997), p. 9.
37 Wolfhart Pannenberg, *Systematic Theology, Volume 2* (Eerdmans, 1994), p. 37.
38 Seraphim Sigrist, *Theology of Wonder* (St Vladimir's Press, 2000), p. 4.
39 Deane-Drummond, *Wonder and Wisdom*, p. 41.
40 Arthur Peacocke, *Creation and the World of Science* (Clarendon, 1979), p. 111.
41 Johan Huizinga, *Homo Ludens: A study of the play-element in culture* (Angelico Press, 2016), p. 1.
42 Rebecca Nye, *Children's Spirituality: What it is and why it matters* (Church House Publishing, 2009), p. 78.
43 Jürgen Moltmann, *Theology and Joy* (SCM, 1973), p. 39.
44 Robert K. Johnson, *The Christian at Play* (Eerdmans, 1983), p. 146.
45 Hayes, *Bonaventure*, pp. 978, 1022.
46 Robert, Ellis, *The Games People Play: Theology, religion, and sport* (Wipf and Stock, 2014), p. 144.
47 Berger, *A Rumour of Angels*, p. 75.
48 Viladesau, *Theological Aesthetics*, p. 6.

49 Zachary Hayes, *Works of St Bonaventure: On the reduction of the arts to theology* (Franciscan Institute Publications, 1996), p. 12.
50 David Wilkinson, *Christian Eschatology and the Phyiscal Universe* (T&T Clarke, 2010), p. 14.
51 Wolfhart Pannenberg, *Systematic Theology, Volume 3* (Eerdmans, 1998), p. 589.
52 Keith Ward, *God, Chance and Necessity* (OneWorld, 1996), pp. 50–51.
53 John C. Polkinghorne, *Science and the Trinity: The Christian encounter with reality* (SPCK, 2004), p. 81.
54 The left part of the image is taken in light with wavelengths of 304 Angstroms, the centre, 193 Angstroms, and the right, 171 Angstroms. An Angstrom is a unit of measurement used in studies of light. Ten Angstroms equals a nanometre, a billionth of a metre. To help get an idea of how small this is, a human hair is about 100,000 nanometres wide.
55 Oxygen in the Earth's atmosphere exists as pairs of atoms – O_2. Ozone is made up of three oxygen atoms – O_3.
56 *Magnificent Desolation* is the title of Buzz Aldrin's autobiography (Bloomsbury, 2009).
57 Elizabeth Howell, 'ISS astronauts witness "spectacular" auroras from space', 25 February 2024, **space.com/iss-aurora-solar-maximum-astronaut-surprise**.

This series of reflections lets scientific discoveries fuel your worship and helps you to consider how we can move forward wisely in a scientific society. Written by a diverse group of scientists and theologians associated with the Faraday Institute for Science and Religion in Cambridge, UK, you are invited into the conversation whether you are a scientist or not, and you are given the opportunity to respond in both praise and practical action.

The Works of the Lord
52 biblical reflections on science, technology and creation
Edited by Ruth Bancewicz
978 1 80039 285 4 £12.99
brfonline.org.uk

In *Reflected by Nature* Claire Daniel offers 40 Bible-themed reflections inspired by the natural world, ten for each season, alongside original artwork by Jamie Poole. This gentle companion to contemplation will help you reflect on God every day, in every season of the year.

Reflected in Nature
Finding God in the created world
Claire Daniels, with illustrations from Jamie Poole
978 0 80039 370 7 £12.99
brfonline.org.uk

Available from September 2025

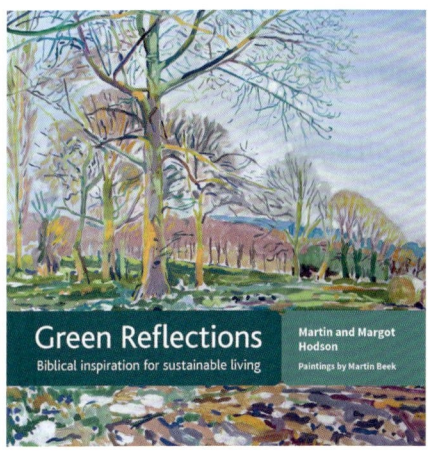

How should we look after the world we inhabit? Martin and Margot Hodson bring together scientific and theological wisdom to offer 62 reflections inspired by passages from the Bible in a thoughtful exploration that encourages both reflection and response. Themes include The Wisdom of Trees, Landscapes of Promise and Sharing Resources.

Green Reflections
Biblical inspiration for sustainable living
Martin and Margot Hodson
978 1 80039 068 3 £8.99
brfonline.org.uk

...to grow in Christian faith

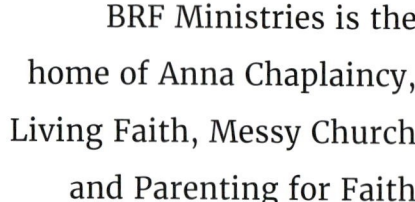

BRF Ministries is the home of Anna Chaplaincy, Living Faith, Messy Church and Parenting for Faith

As a charity, our work would not be possible without fundraising and gifts in wills. To find out more and to donate, visit brf.org.uk/give or call +44 (0)1235 462305